The Thoughts in My Head

LISA LEVY

You Can Only Call It Art If You're an Artist...
In Conversation with Lisa Levy by Jane Ursula Harris

In 1986, Lisa Levy appeared on David Letterman's "Stupid Pet Tricks" with her hamster, Bitey, in what she now sees as her first performance artwork, "Hamster Bowling." Holding Bitey inside a hamster exercise ball, Levy explains her trick to Letterman, "she's gonna bowl."

"So in essence we're saying goodbye to Bitey tonite," Letterman quips back to loud audience laughter.

Dressed in a turquoise top replete with shoulder pads and black leggings, and donning a gamine-style haircut, Levy doesn't miss a beat. "No way!" she replies. "She loves it!"

And true enough, after being set down on the floor in front of a set of colorful plastic bowling pins, Bitey comes rolling along as Levy calls her, knocking down a couple along the way. It's hilarious and adorable, and you can watch it on the artist's YouTube channel.

The year 1986 is also when Levy made her first artwork, a pair of his-and-her silk-screen signs mimicking the kind posted in bathrooms that exhort employees to wash their hands. In her version, there are outlines of a female body and a male body with arrows pointing to their hands in a parody of the obvious. "I was making fun of them by making them dumber" she tells me. Levy posted them guerilla-style everywhere she went for months, taping them up in the bathrooms

of bars, restaurants, clubs, and art spaces. "Every time I went back to a place to check on them, they were stolen, even on the next day."

Like "Hamster Bowling," Levy didn't consider these actions art at the time because as an art director working in advertising, she didn't consider herself an artist yet. The art world, as everyone knows, gate-keeps in ways that can make anyone feel like an imposter; you can only call it art if you're an artist. Not surprising then that during these early years she didn't have the confidence to consider these acts "art" with a capital "A." Something tells me Andy Kaufman would've though, because in many ways Kaufman's brand of offbeat humor is the perfect precedent for Levy's vision of art as comedy and comedy as performance art.

Why am I going all the way back to 1986 to discuss a body of work made in the last decade, you might ask? Well, precisely because it illustrates just how refreshingly out-of-the-box Levy's ideas about art have been since the beginning—ideas that still permeate the series that comprises this book, *Thoughts Inside My Head*. Like the cheeky postcards Levy made when she checked herself into a depression clinic for six weeks A Photo for Today, 1993; the matchbook edition she made commemorating her first period, My First Period Matches, 1994; and the "Studio 54 Reject" T-shirts she sold outside the club in 1978 and then again outside the Brooklyn Museum of Art's Studio 54: Night

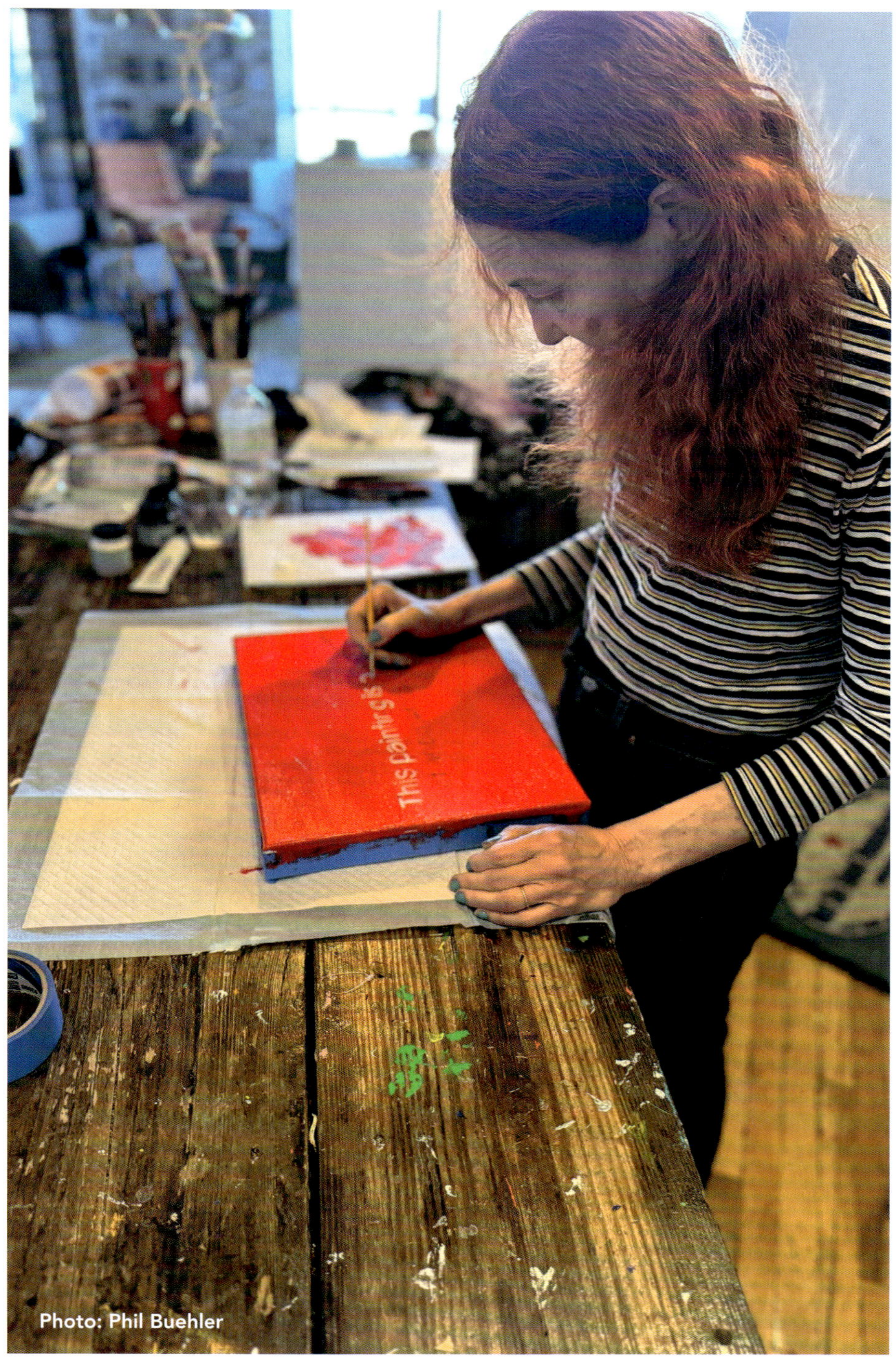

Photo: Phil Buehler

Magic exhibition (2020), her relationship to art and language has always been remarkably—and paradoxically—personal yet self-effacing. Consider that both times she performed naked on stage, she did so in ways that were deliberately unflattering. There was her infamous work, *The Artist Is Humbly Present*, January, 2016, a send-up of the Marina Abramovic performance at MoMA, where she sat on a toilet across from another toilet inviting anyone who wanted to to sit across from her, and well, stare. And more recently, she performed a monologue around a series of body scars and their effect on her life (*Traveling in My Body Through Time*, 2019).

This is an artist who isn't afraid to expose herself if it means being seen and connecting to others. Call it a kind of unwitting neurotic exhibitionism driven by a childhood in which she mostly felt invisible, but Levy uses vulnerability as a medium, bravely peddling her insecurities and insights to make people think and laugh as comedians have always done. In the titular series, *Thoughts Inside My Head*, (2011) this takes the form of witticisms, advice, declarations, inner dialogue, aphorisms, and other hilariously, often poignant thoughts that have been reduced—like the perfect ad slogan—to a single sentence.Each is painted onto flat color fields in a kind of painterly drag that refuses to take itself too seriously while still boldly revealing what most keep hidden inside; two hallmarks that I think also distinguish Levy's work with text and language. Who else would feel comfortable publicizing slogans that read, "Motherhood seems like slavery to me" and "I'm comfortable with how neurotic I am"? It takes guts and lots and lots of therapy, LOL, which Levy has undergone enough of that she can now shrink herself and others as well. Ask Dr. Lisa, Self-proclaimed Psychotherapist, a persona she's inhabited for years, one that's also enabled her to finally realize she's not only an artist, but as she would say of others, the "real deal."

What follows is my attempt to "shrink" the shrink as we discuss what was behind some of the works that comprise this book and talk about the series.

JUH: I thought we could start with "No one loves you like your parents, including your parents." I feel like it conveys a kind of existential loneliness that many of us feel, especially those who've been disappointed by our parents. It's from 2017, I think, right? Wasn't that the year of your solo exhibition, "Get My Stuff When I am Dead," where you offered up all your prized possessions to those who wanted them? I thought that was a really powerful show about facing one's death and also a moving story about your life through "stuff." Any links between where your head was at for the show—I know it coincided with your having turned 60—and the painting's slogan?

LL: That show was actually an expansion of a project that I redid from 1997 near my 40th birthday titled, "I'm Taking Stock of the Situation," which was exhibited at White Columns. At the time, whenever people came to my home, I had them choose a possession of mine that they wanted to be put in my will for them. Then I would take their photo and add their name/object to a checklist putting a red dot on their chosen object, etc. I even worked with The Volunteer Lawyers for the Arts to make a legal will too.

But yes, the 2017 show really allowed me to explore death as one of the most powerful motivating factors behind our actions yet one most of us don't acknowledge openly. And it was a cleansing of emotions and memories for me that helped me reframe a lot of my personal history to see myself in a more positive light. And that painting, "No one loves you like your parents, including your parents" sort of acknowledges that effort. I had a difficult childhood, I didn't feel welcome in my family, and we certainly never talked about death in a serious way. My mother wanted to donate her body to science and my dad would say, "She's going chicken by the parts." Also, a lot of themes in my text paintings deal with mothers, motherhood, and parenting because I spent so much of my adult life trying to repair the damage from my childhood. So, when I turned 60 I began thinking about the end of my life, and that painting, like the exhibition I did the same year, was a way to continue to recognize and undo the self-destructive behavior and low self-esteem I'd internalized growing up.

JUH: It makes me think of another work, "I wish I was suicidal so I wouldn't be afraid of dying" that I'd categorize as one of your more controversial statements (like the two mentioned in my intro). One could put "There is no shame in shame" in that category too. Can you talk about these sorts of thoughts and what putting them out there means for you?

LL: You know, I was censored by an angry curator for "Motherhood is like slavery to me." I don't necessarily anticipate a particular painting will be controversial when I make it. When I did "There is no shame in shame" I was trying to say that we all have shame: I constantly fear I will feel shame about the work I put out, including the message in that work! At the same time, making the painting was a way to self-soothe, and to try and connect with people to reassure them that the shame they are feeling may or may not be based in truth, and like mine, is probably just born out of insecurities. I feel that shame is often an obstacle to people connecting.

But I really can't guess how people will react to any one painting until it's out there and I am often surprised at the reactions. I think that in a collection of 100 paintings, I wouldn't be doing my job if some weren't controversial. I think my mission is to express the thoughts I have that I don't see out in the world. When people respond to the work, I feel the connection that I'm looking for, though it's not always positive.

JUH: Absolutely, that's what makes them interesting. What would you say are the crowd pleasers?

LL: Probably works like: "I don't know who you are, but I need your approval"; "I'm a really uptight free spirit"; "If I've never offended you, we're not that close"; "Permanent is still temporary", "We hung this painting here to cover a hole"; and "I think you probably could have made this but you didn't."

JUH: The latter is one of my favorites as it seems to embody the spirit of the series and your attitude toward the art world as do others like "You can tell how well your art career is going by who says hello to you at the openings", and "Charles Saatchi, this painting has your name on it!".

LL: I have a love/hate relationship to the art world. I love some of the art that is out there, but I am put off by the pretentiousness and the way some artists and art world people take themselves so seriously—the air of exclusivity that dominates. Some art is hard to understand like poetry or opera, except that day to day, we live with it—even in hotel rooms. I think Maurizio Cattelan summed it up best in "Comedian" which was an artwork of a banana taped to a wall. It's funny because it's so apparent anyone could have made it, but if he wasn't such a well-respected artist, no one would have cared. The work sold for $120,000. But with those two you mention, I think they reflect my exaggerated fear of authority. I was always afraid of my parents and of adults in general growing up, and it still haunts me today. Even though I am older than most of the authority figures I encounter in the art world now, I am conscious of people who, whatever role they are in, have higher status than me. There was a time when I would go to an art opening and be shaking to get the nerve to talk to people that had more status—usually just other artists. The flip side is a drive to please. At the time, Charles Saatchi was the figure I would most have wanted approval from. Of course, I am also making fun of myself and the system at the same time.

JUH: I love that! It's all part of this pseudodiaristic quality that animates the works in *Thoughts in My Head*, especially when they address issues of self-esteem. Is making them cathartic for you beyond self-soothing?

LL: They can be very cathartic. in ways that allow me to connect to people and feel a kinship with the viewer. It feels good, for example, when I see a polished looking woman whom I find intimidating clearly relate to: "I feel like an uptight free spirit." Some reactions to paintings surprise me though, in terms of what people respond to and what they don't. Like everyone seems to identify with "Don't take it personally is always good advice" and "Money obscures feelings" don't necessarily evoke the reaction I thought they might.

JUH: Well, as you've suggested, the responses can be unpredictable. Is this different than when you perform?

LL: Yes, because my relationship to the viewer is so different. When I make these paintings, I have little chance to experience people's response as I'm not there in the gallery, so I don't have that way of connecting that's visceral. When I plan a performance, I have a goal or a message and when I'm doing the performance, I get a sense of what the audience is experiencing, and I can use that in the moment to deepen my connection with them. But sometimes I use performance to interact with people where my physical presence isn't part of it. Like leaving the "Employees Must Wash Hands." posters in public bathrooms. Or when I made cement cow turds and glued them under those horrible public sculpture cows around the city. And another of set of postcards I made, Art and Commerce, 1993, featuring me naked holding signs that say things like, "I appear vulnerable"; "I'm looking for your approval" and "Pay for my art and you can think of it as pornography."

JUH: What's the criteria for a phrase or comment making it into a painting versus being an idea for a performance?

LL: Since *The Thoughts in My Head* is an ongoing work, I write notes to myself on my phone regularly when ideas for paintings come up. When I am about to do an exhibition, I go to my file of what I have saved and start editing. Performances and my other work start from a similar conceptual place—from an idea I want to get out. The execution comes out of the concept, not one technique or method. I see this collection of paintings in total as one robustly realized concept.

The Thoughts in My Head series has had a lasting impact on the actual thoughts in my head. Making and exhibiting the works over a ten-year period has been a roller coaster of feelings which include failure, success, embarrassment, anger, disappointment, joy, intimacy, self-discovery—I could go on. I have had commissions with this series, which has given me the opportunity to get close to people and help express the thoughts in their head. And now I'm given the opportunity to do this book. I'm proud of being able to generate a life experience which has helped me grow in the most positive way. And that's something I can genuinely be proud of.

ARTIST STATEMENT

I have always been an overthinker. And that has mostly brought me confusion, depression, and a feeling of being overwhelmed, often by imaginary scenarios and conversations. I grew up in a family of four in a small apartment with thin walls, often hearing my mother complaining about me to my father. For some of that I don't blame her. Fortunately, she never found out about my driving the family car high on LSD while I was in high school (pardon the pun).

Hearing my parents talk about me in a less than positive way was a factor that led me to a heightened awareness of what I was thinking along with a tug of war in my head; I was always trying to discern the difference between what was real and what I was imagining as what my parents would be saying. The Thoughts in My Head denotes a healing vote of self-confidence in the way I am making a commitment to my own thoughts as a work of art.

In my twenties, influenced by my job as an art director in advertising as well as Jenny Holzer's truisms, I began putting text on objects. They were sold at the Exit Art and The New Museum bookstores. The text reflected a message that was inspired by the object. For example, text on an iron said, "You can't straighten out your life by ironing your clothes." I silkscreened, "Put yourself in my shoes" onto socks. Boomerangs said, "I'd like to get rid of my insecurities." And on my bathroom scale was written, "Meter of self-loathing."

After a while, I had thoughts that didn't flow from an object, and so they needed to be out there on their own. I began to think, well, using a painting as an object presents the words as "Art," and that's the context of how I wanted people to receive these words.

I further developed these text paintings at a Byrdcliffe artist residency in June 2011. Over the next ten years, the original collection of a dozen paintings grew into more than one hundred. The number of lines I've written is likely ten to twenty times more than that as I write constantly, sending myself notes on my phone.

The Thoughts in My Head series exceeded my expectations—it has been exhibited at many art fairs and galleries, and held in numerous collections. VSOP Projects has represented the work since 2019. I was commissioned to create an installation of text from my paintings as a permanent backdrop to a rooftop pool in San Diego. With this work, I was hired to create a site-specific, text-based installation for the lobby, hallways, bar, and elevators at Yotel, a hotel in Times Square, Manhattan.

I'm gratified in how the series connects directly with people and how it gives that little girl in me great comfort to see how she was never truly alone; That there actually was a lot of humor lurking in her situation, which is so much clearer to me now.

Stepping back, I can see themes in my work—my insecurities about my body, my artwork, my abilities, and my place in the world. Some paintings refer to my relationships, to my family, to my work, and to the world at large. I posit perspectives about society that I feel we ignore. Some of the paintings are self-referential to the painting itself, using the painted canvas as a metaphor for art in general.

The ten-year period during which the work was made is also evident, with references to social media, NFTs, immigration, and the pandemic. I am aware that it is impossible for me to see all the messages that this series expresses to others just as it is impossible for anyone to see themselves the way others see them. I greatly value others' interpretation and I'd love to learn more about my work from them.

Developing this series and my writing skills has also helped me evolve my other work. Most recently, I've worked with a figurative painter, Sharilyn Neidhardt, to create paintings for a sex doll named Skye Cleary, who I anthropomorphized as an artist and exotic dancer. Skye makes paintings to express her feelings about the emotional complexities that comes from a life that straddles the art world and sex worker world. Sharilyn paints the image and I add text later. The visual and text combined posit an idea in each painting. For example, I added "I'm not your therapist" to Sharilyn's painting of sexy, lingerie-clad young women to express that no matter what she does to earn money, Skye is a dedicated artist. I painted "There's nothing I love more than having time to paint" over Sharilyn's painting of a couple having sex. "I love the feeling of power" is painted over another canvas of a woman giving a lap dance. This body of work is more specific with a focus on the power of young women.

While developing this series, I've also ventured into the stand-up comedy world to sharpen my skills at writing humor. For me, stand-up comedy is writing without the artifice of the object.

It is very rewarding for me to see all my text paintings brought together in one book. I hope that people will find the paintings that resonate with them and know someone has been thinking what they have been thinking as proof that they are not alone with those thoughts.

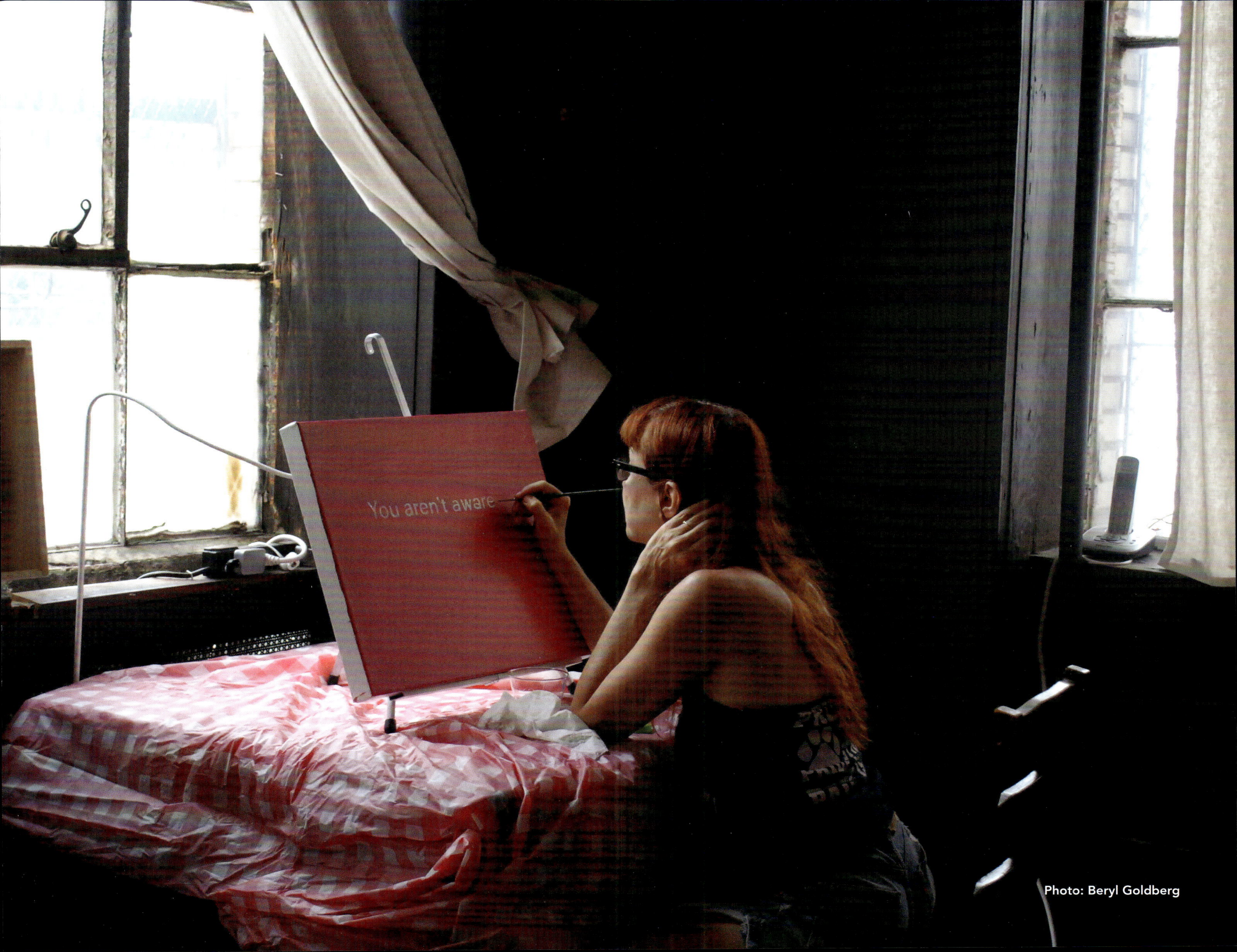

Photo: Beryl Goldberg

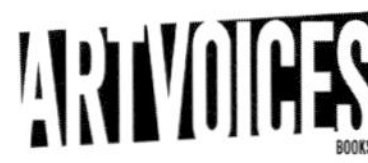

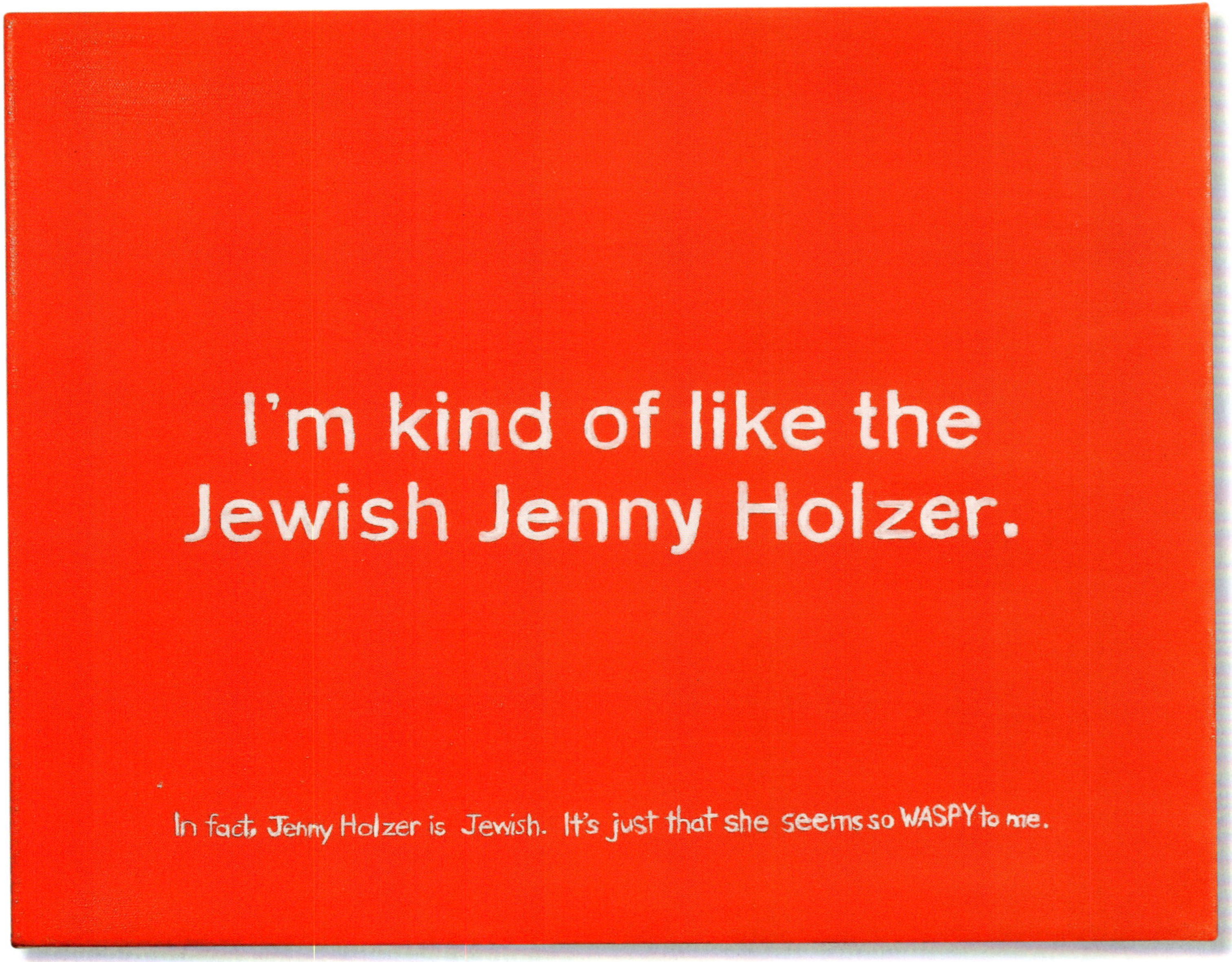

I'm kind of like the
Jewish Jenny Holzer.

In fact, Jenny Holzer is Jewish. It's just that she seems so WASPY to me.

The Thoughts in My Head #1
2011
Acrylic on Canvas
11 x 14 inches

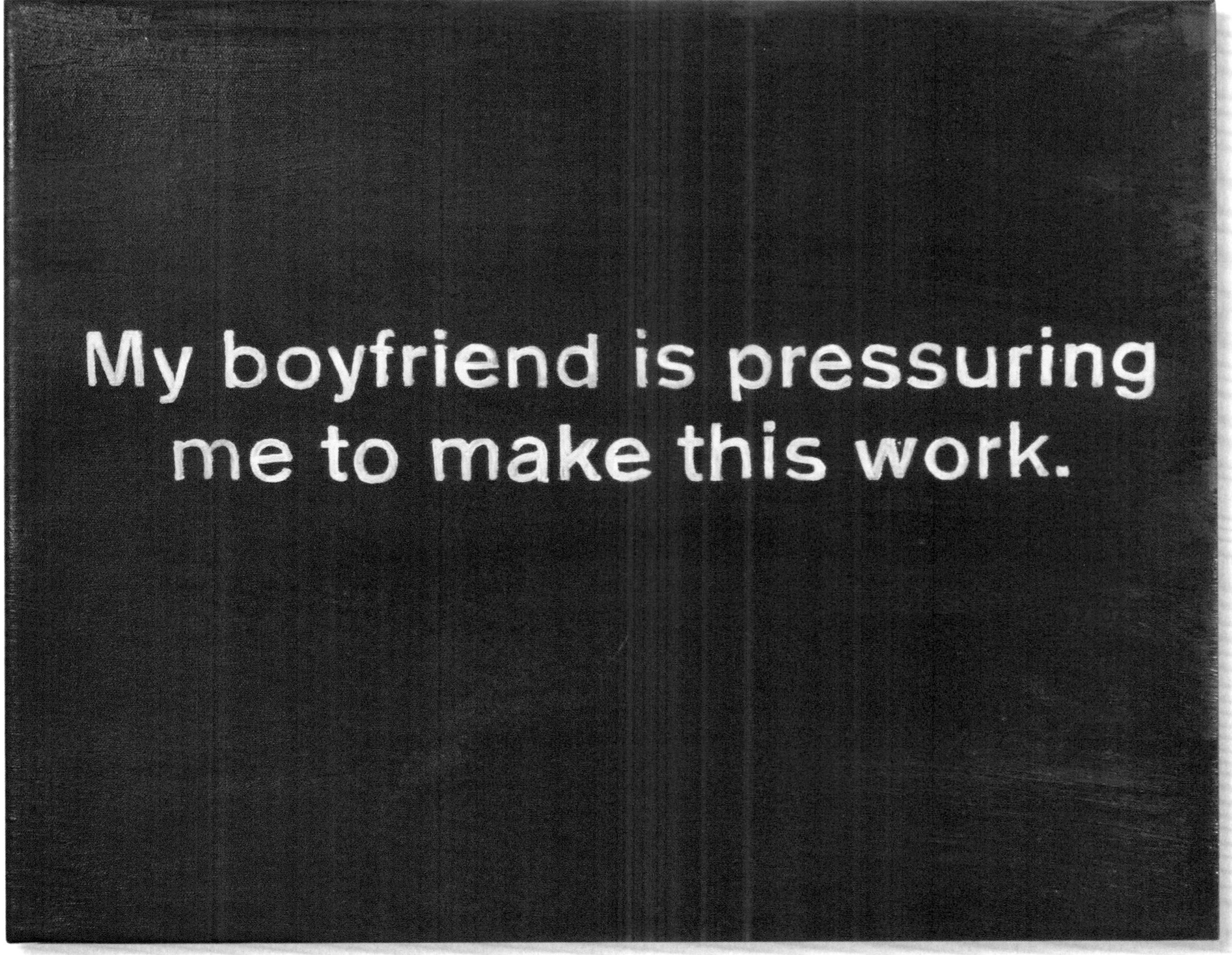

The Thoughts in My Head #2
2011
Acrylic on Canvas
11 x 14 inches

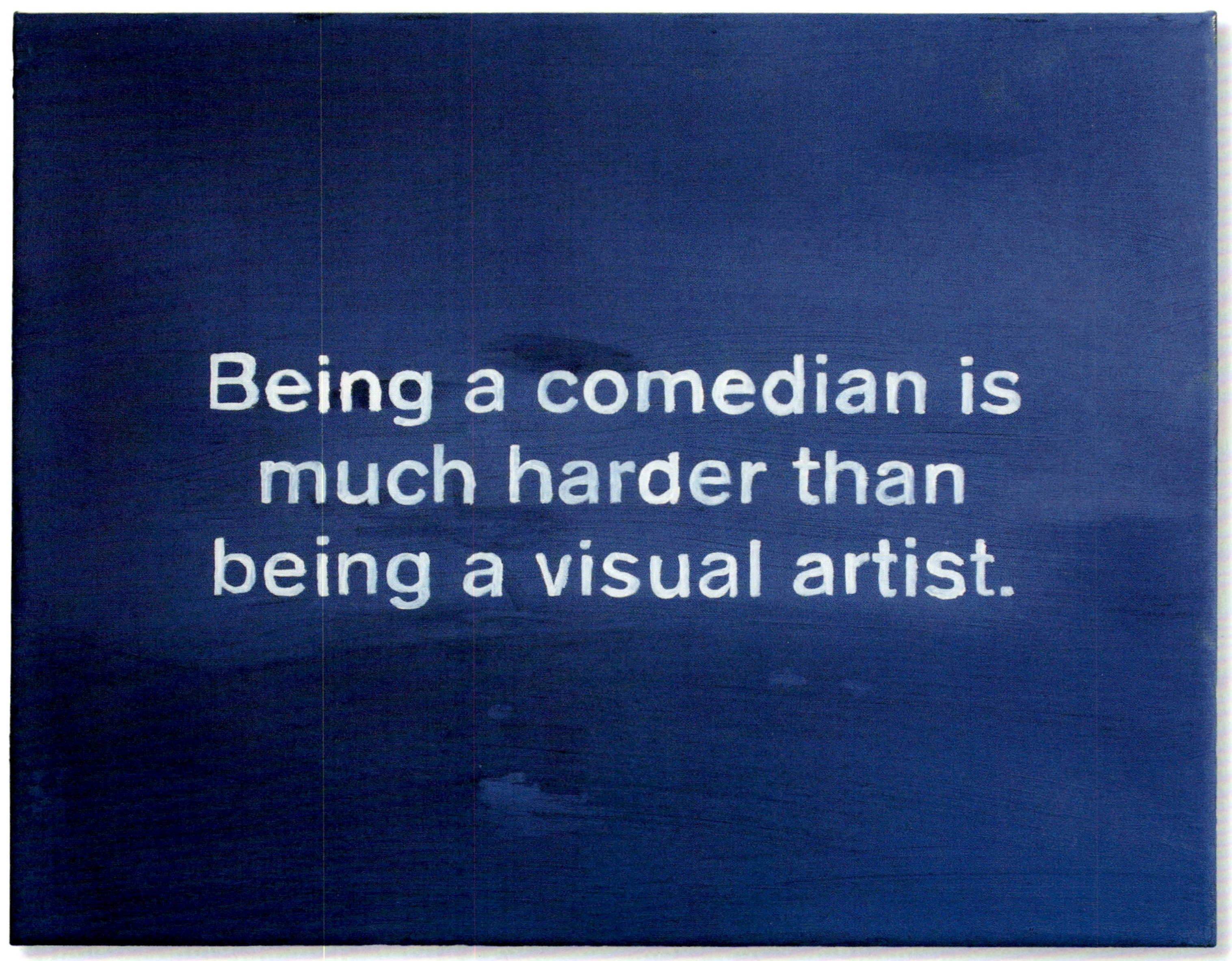

The Thoughts in My Head #3
2011
Acrylic on Canvas
11 x 14 inches

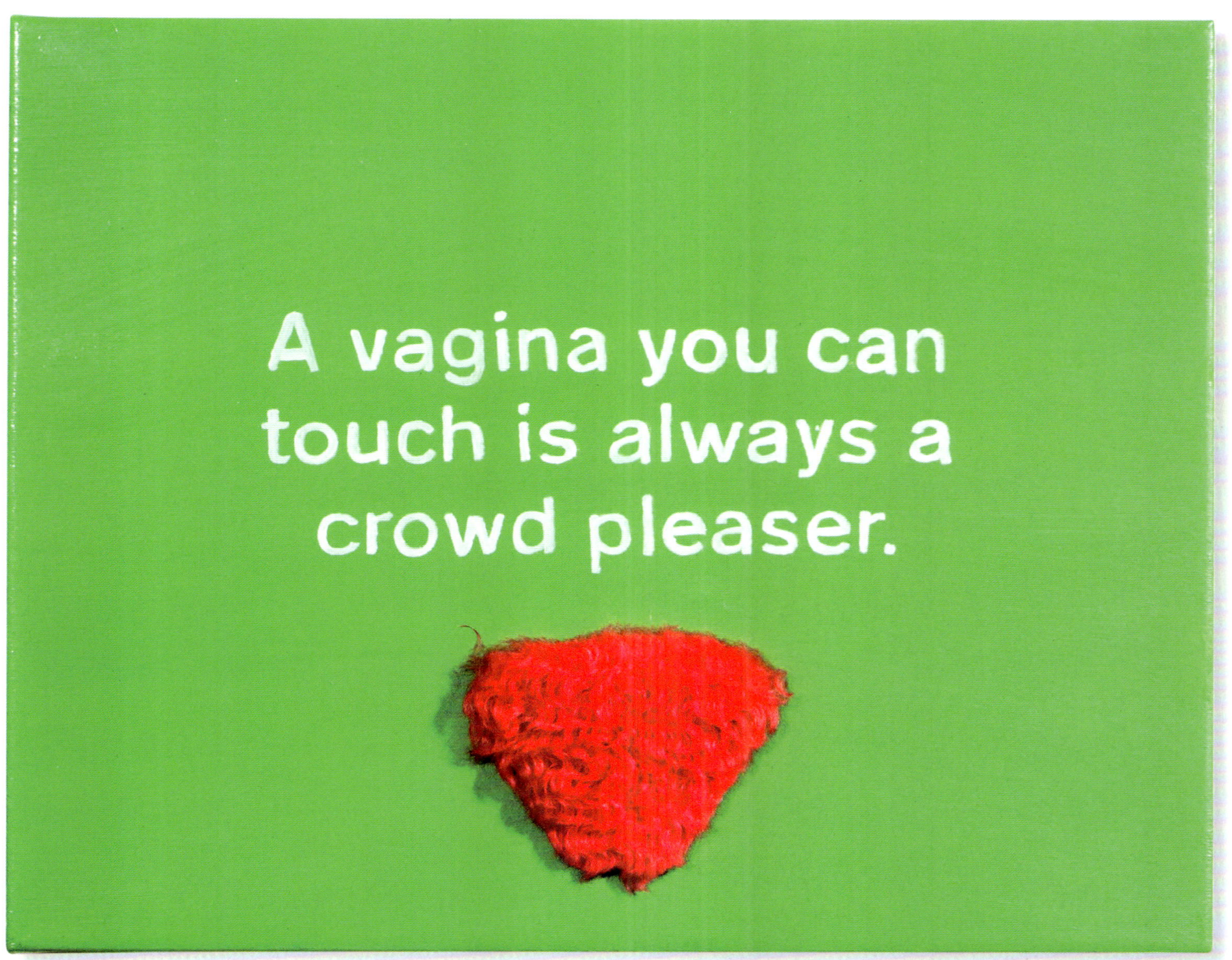

The Thoughts in My Head #4
2011
Acrylic on Canvas
11 x 14 inches

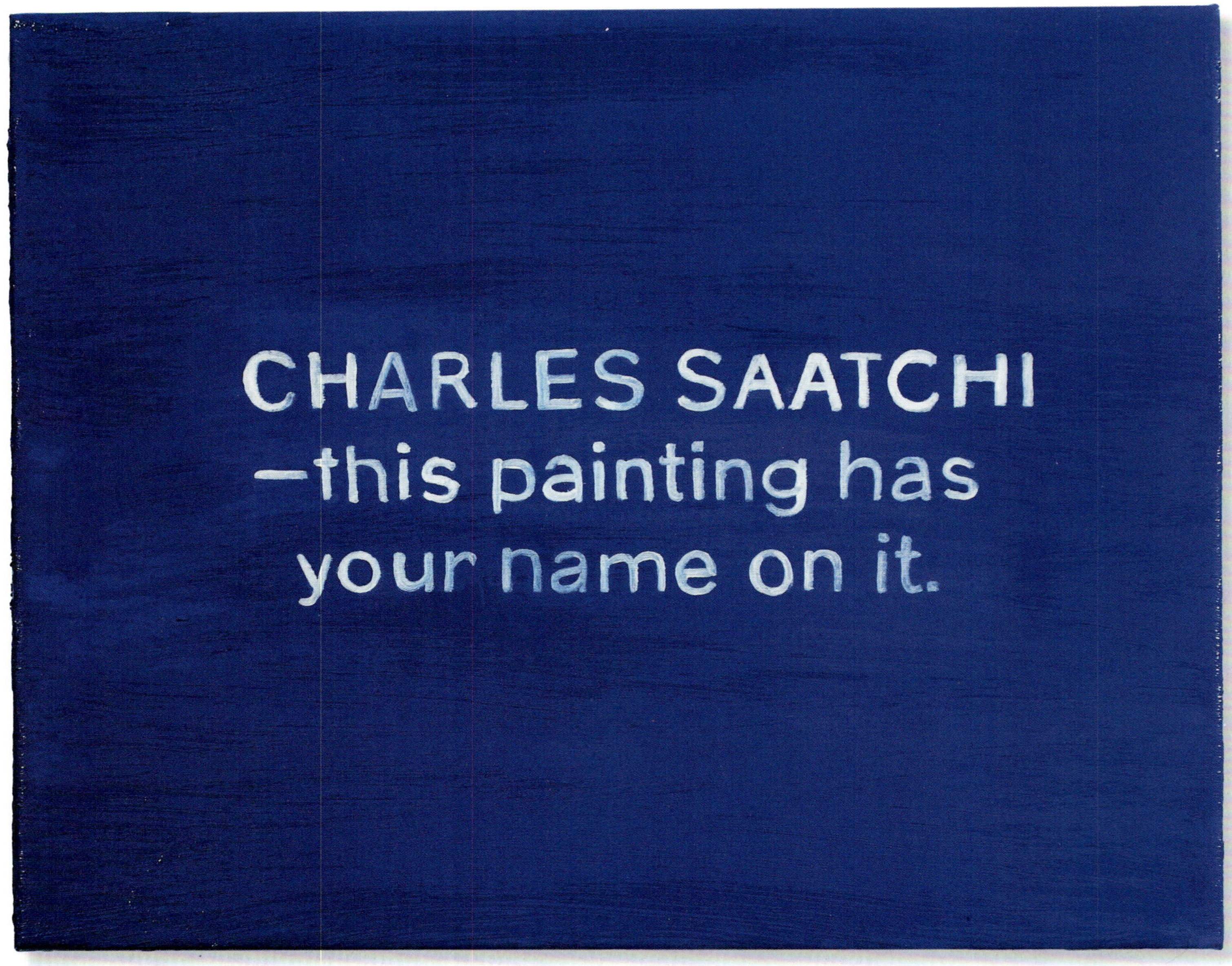

The Thoughts in My Head #5
2011
Acrylic on Canvas
11 x 14 inches

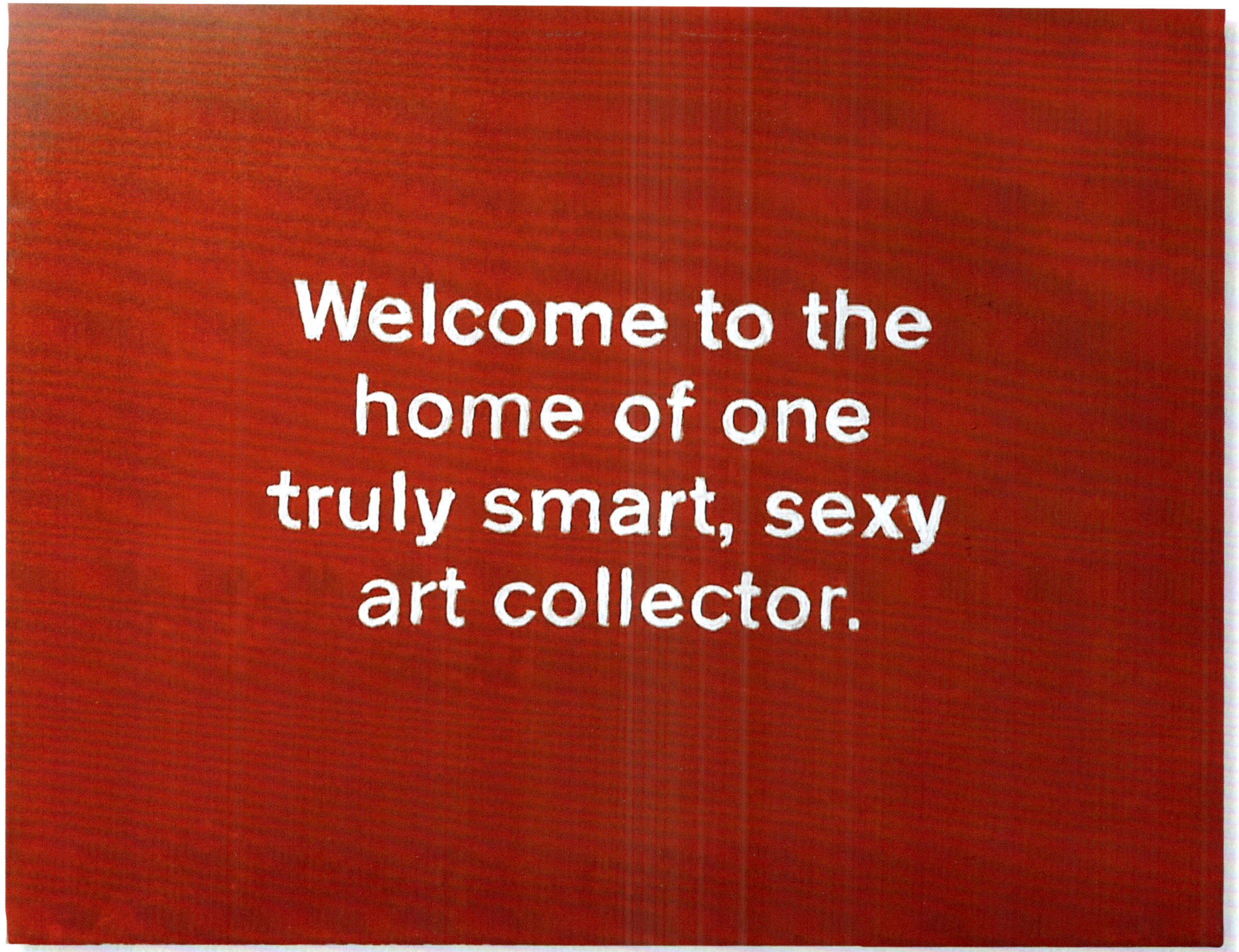

The Thoughts in My Head #6
2011
Acrylic on Canvas
11 x 14 inches

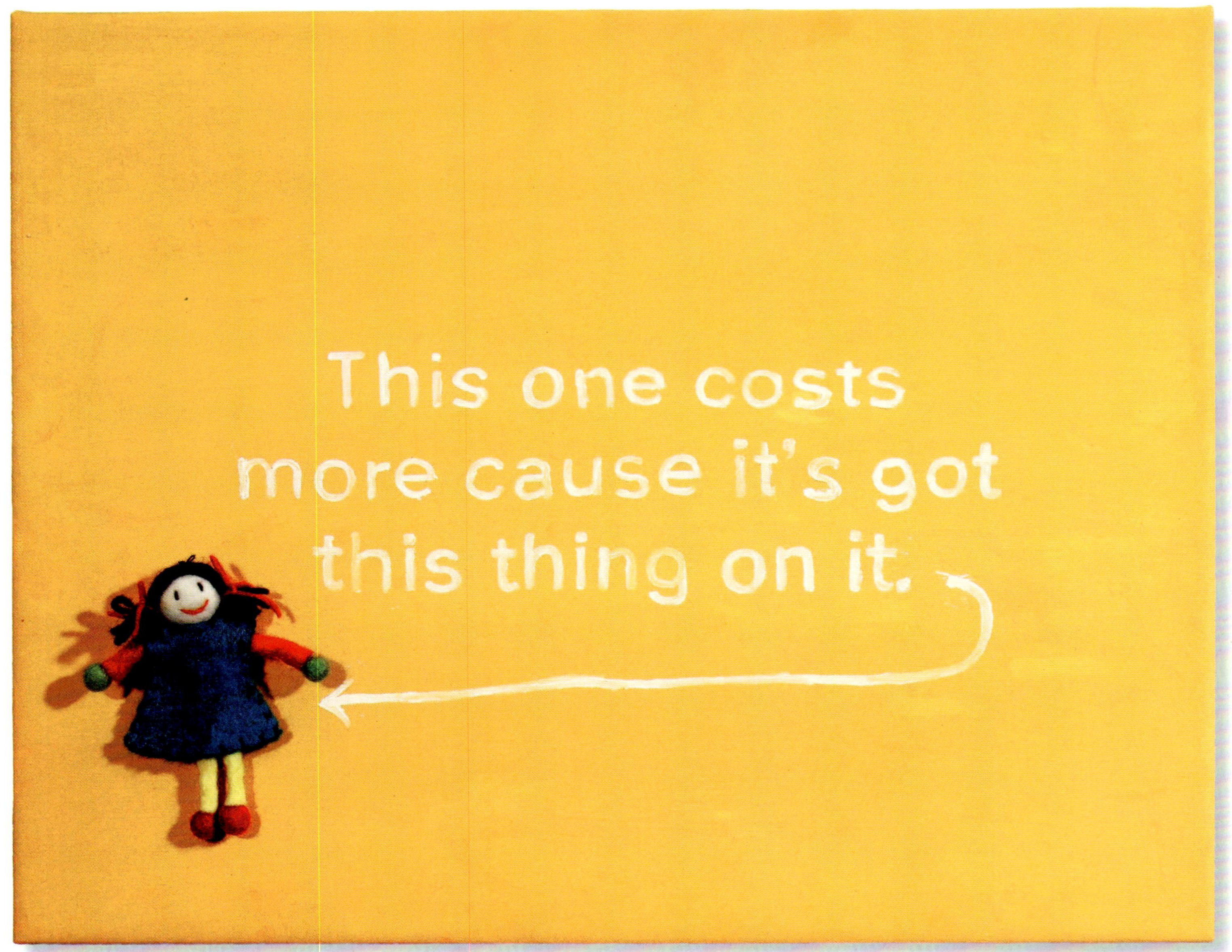

The Thoughts in My Head #7
2011
Acrylic on Canvas
11 x 14 inches

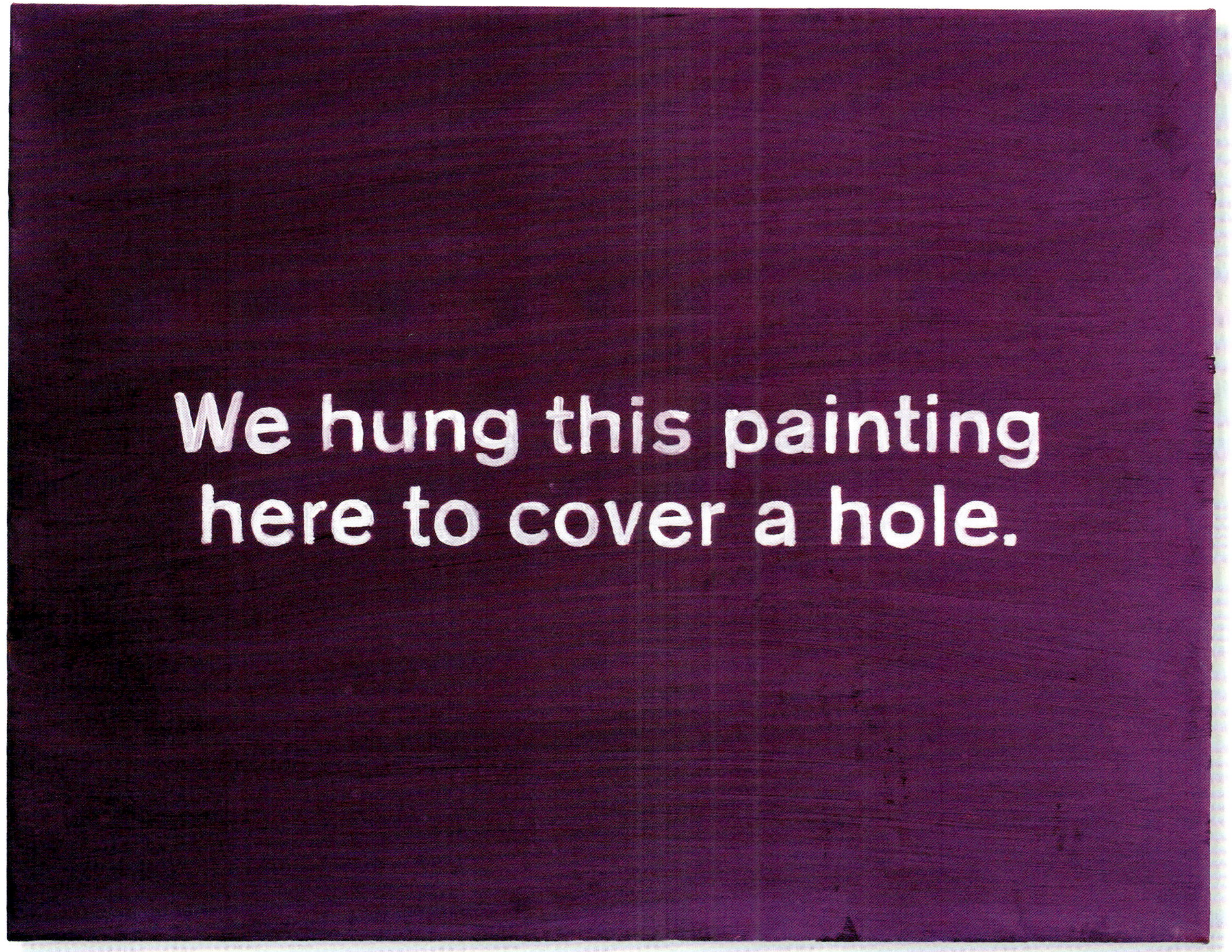

The Thoughts in My Head #8
2011
Acrylic on Canvas
11 x 14 inches

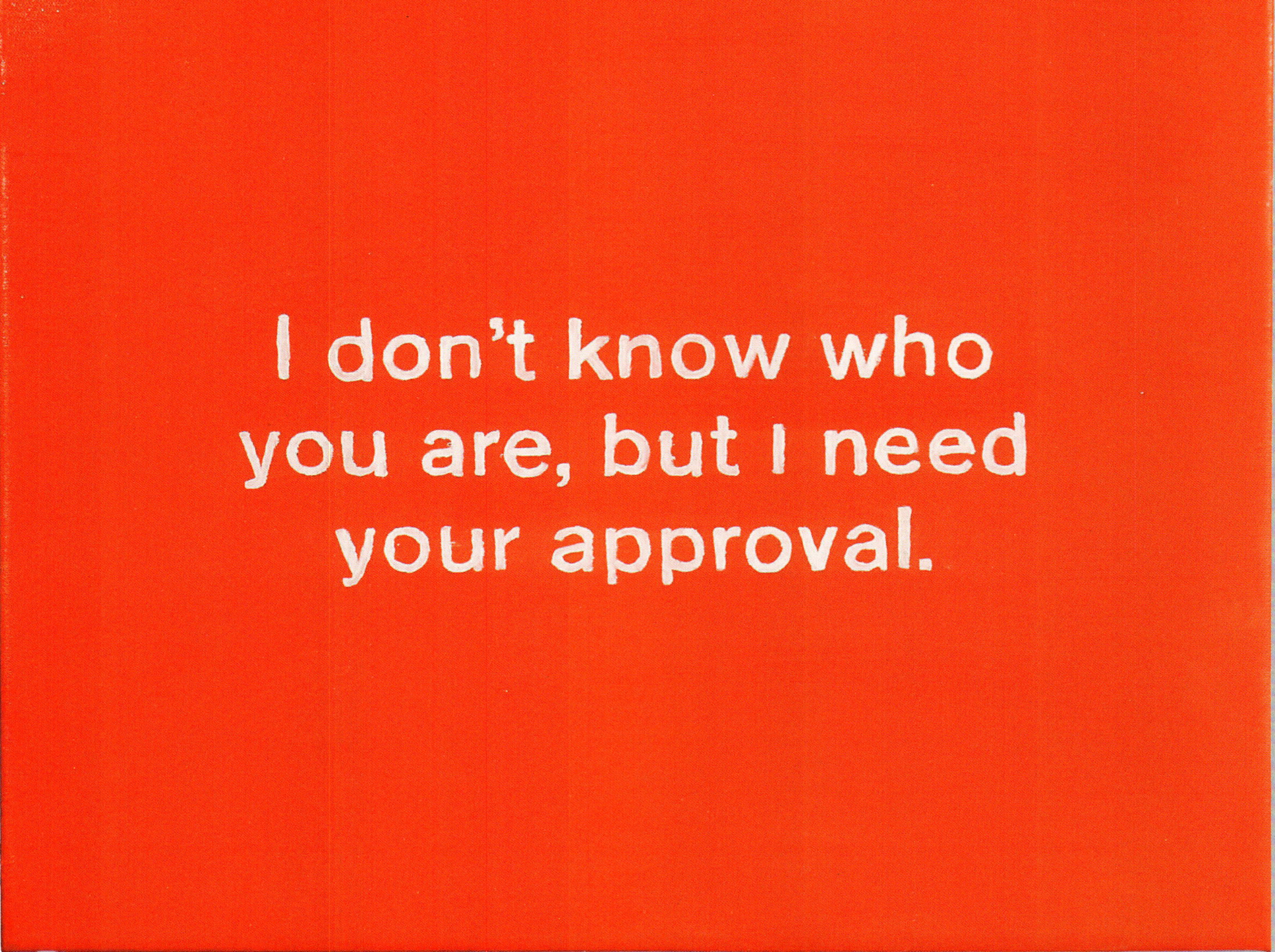

The Thoughts in My Head #9
2011
Acrylic on Canvas
11 x 14 inches

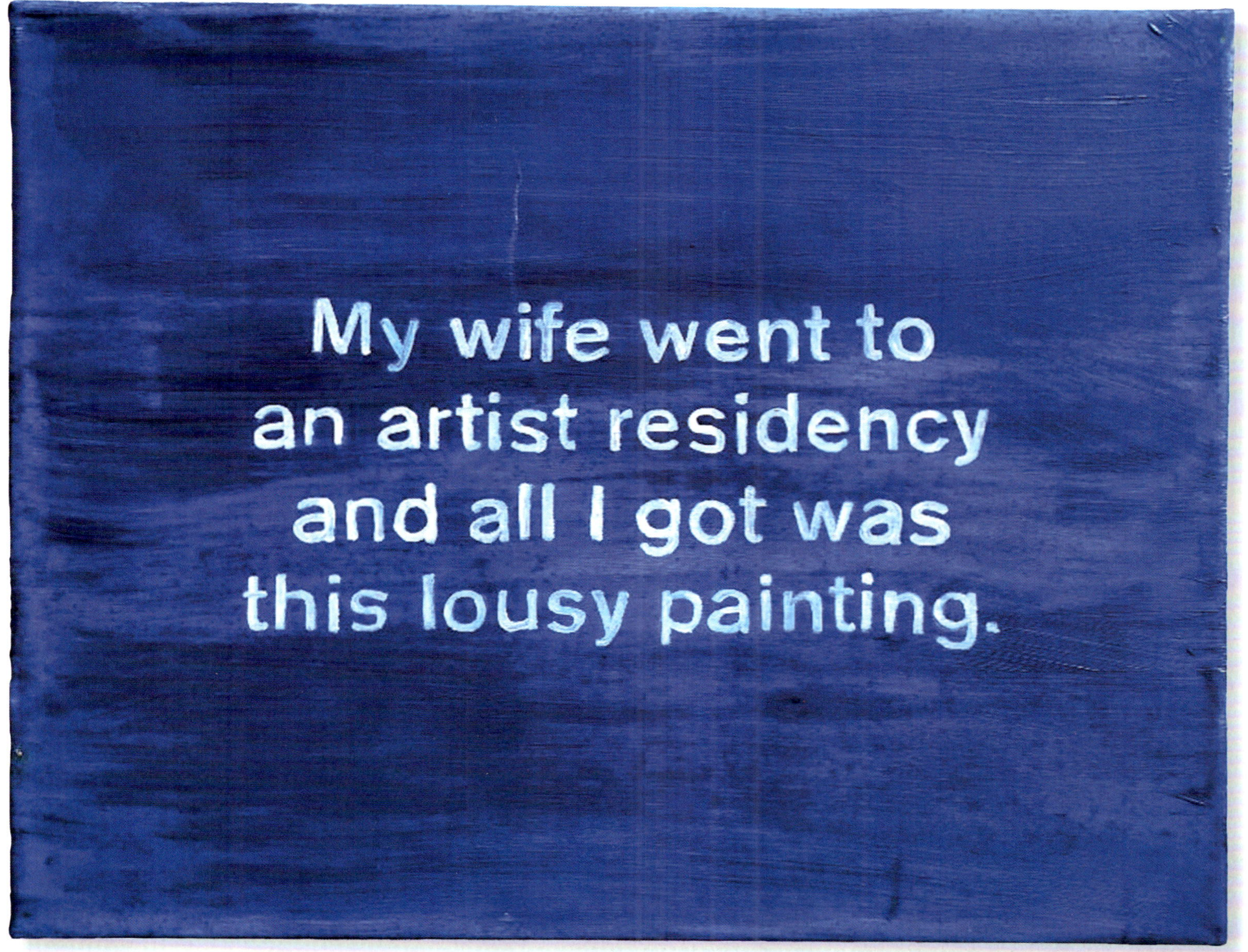

The Thoughts in My Head #10
2011
Acrylic on Canvas
11 x 14 inches

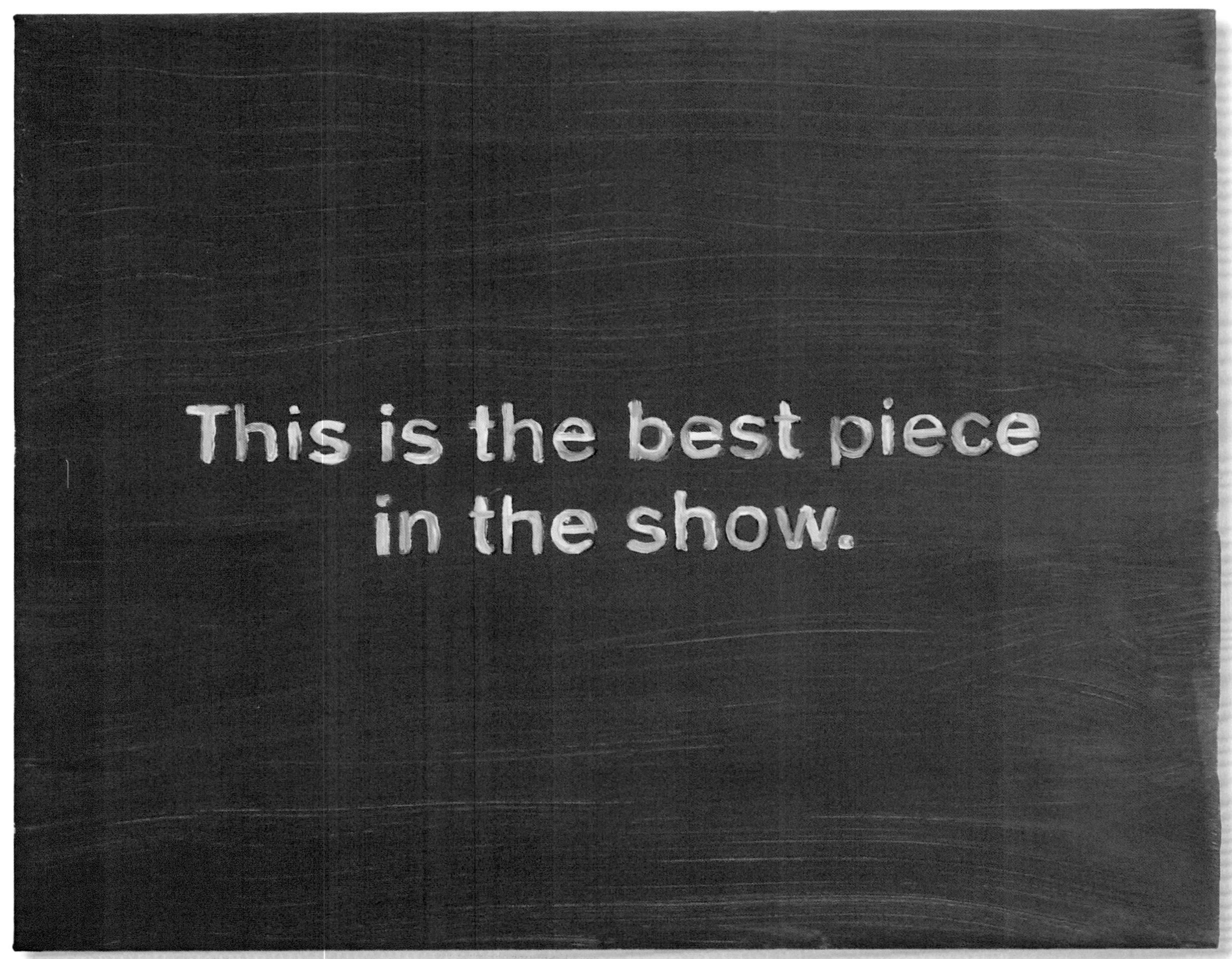

The Thoughts in My Head #11
2011
Acrylic on Canvas
11 x 14 inches

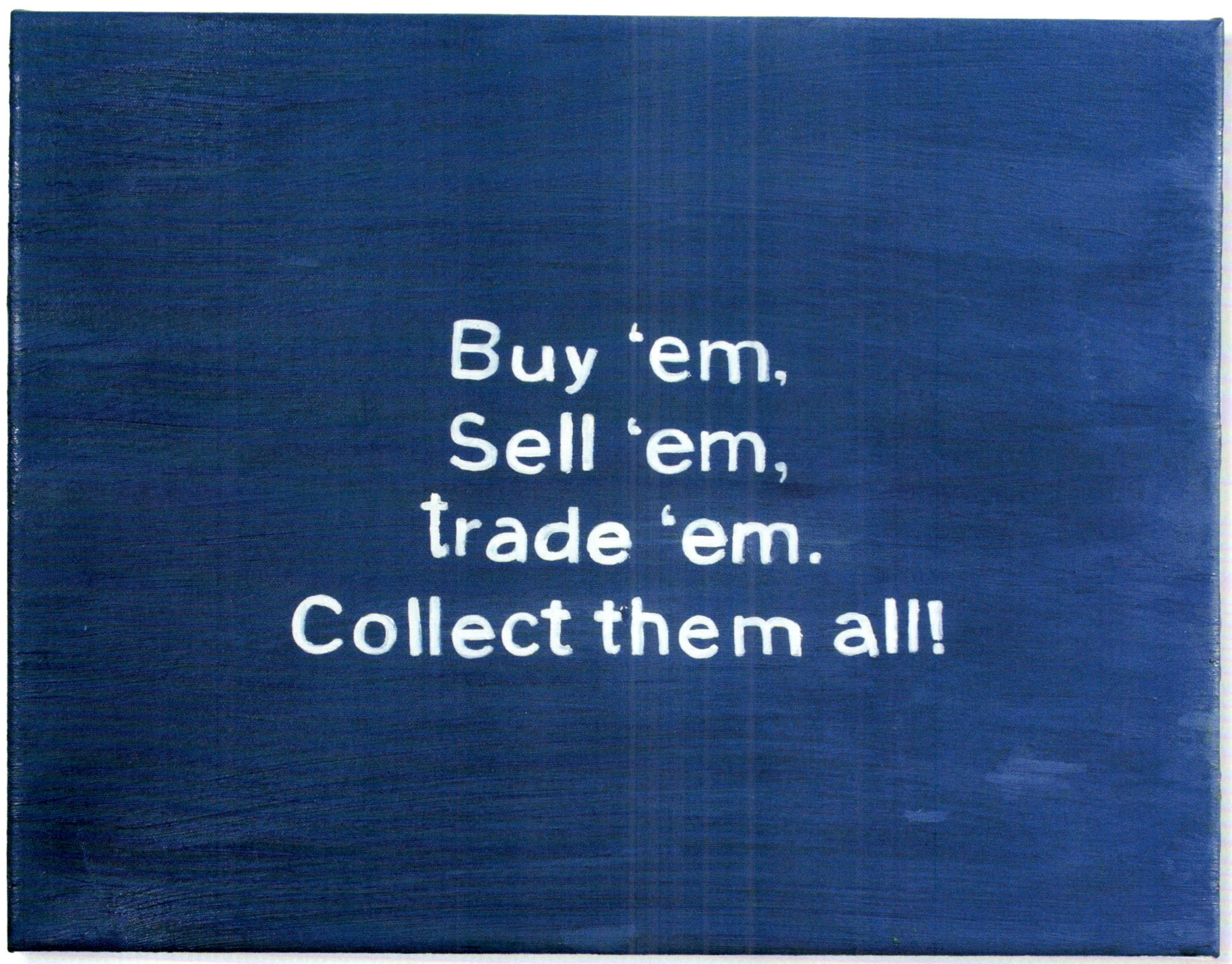

The Thoughts in My Head #12
2011
Acrylic on Canvas
11 x 14 inches

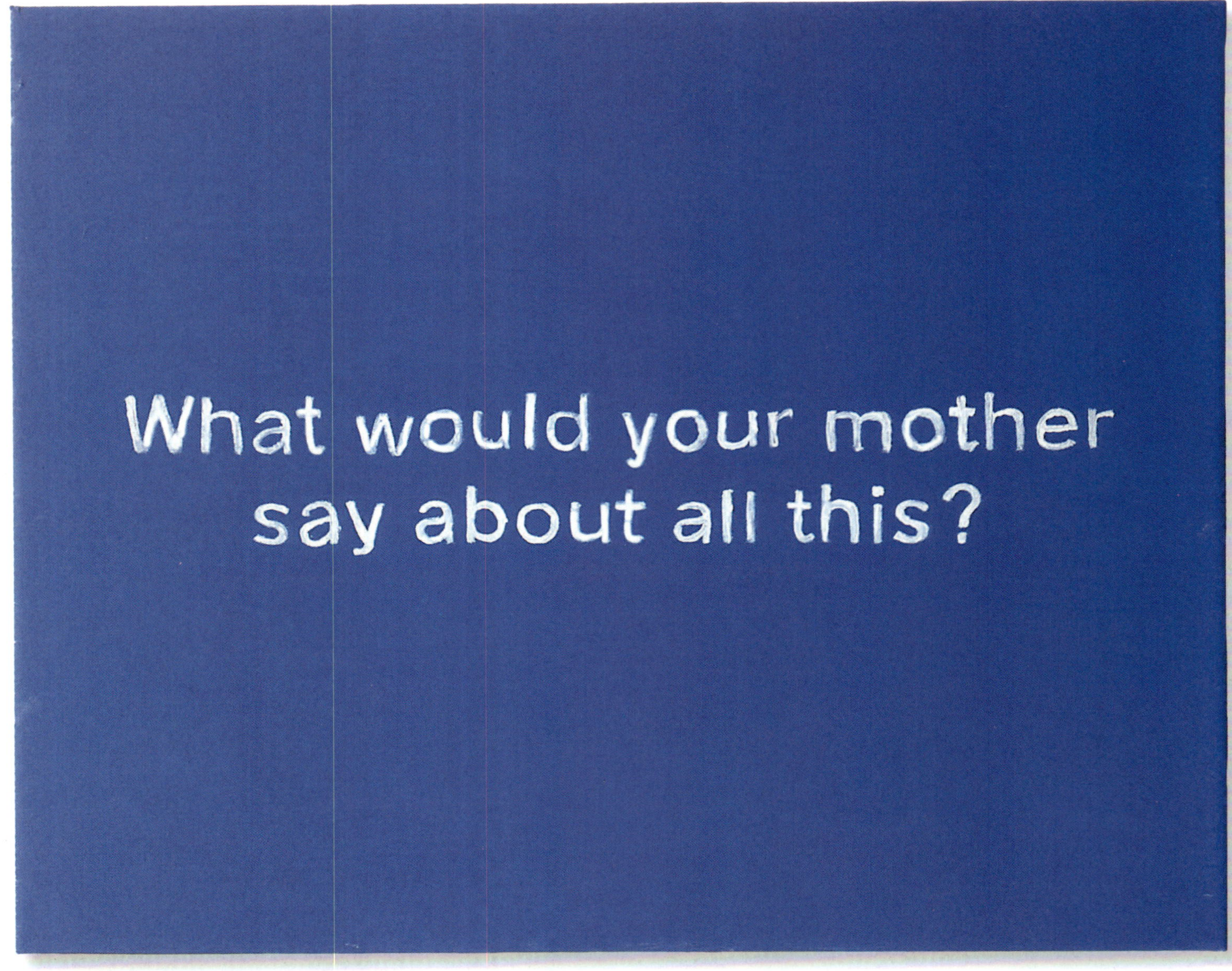

The Thoughts in My Head #13
2012
Acrylic on Canvas
11 x 14 inches

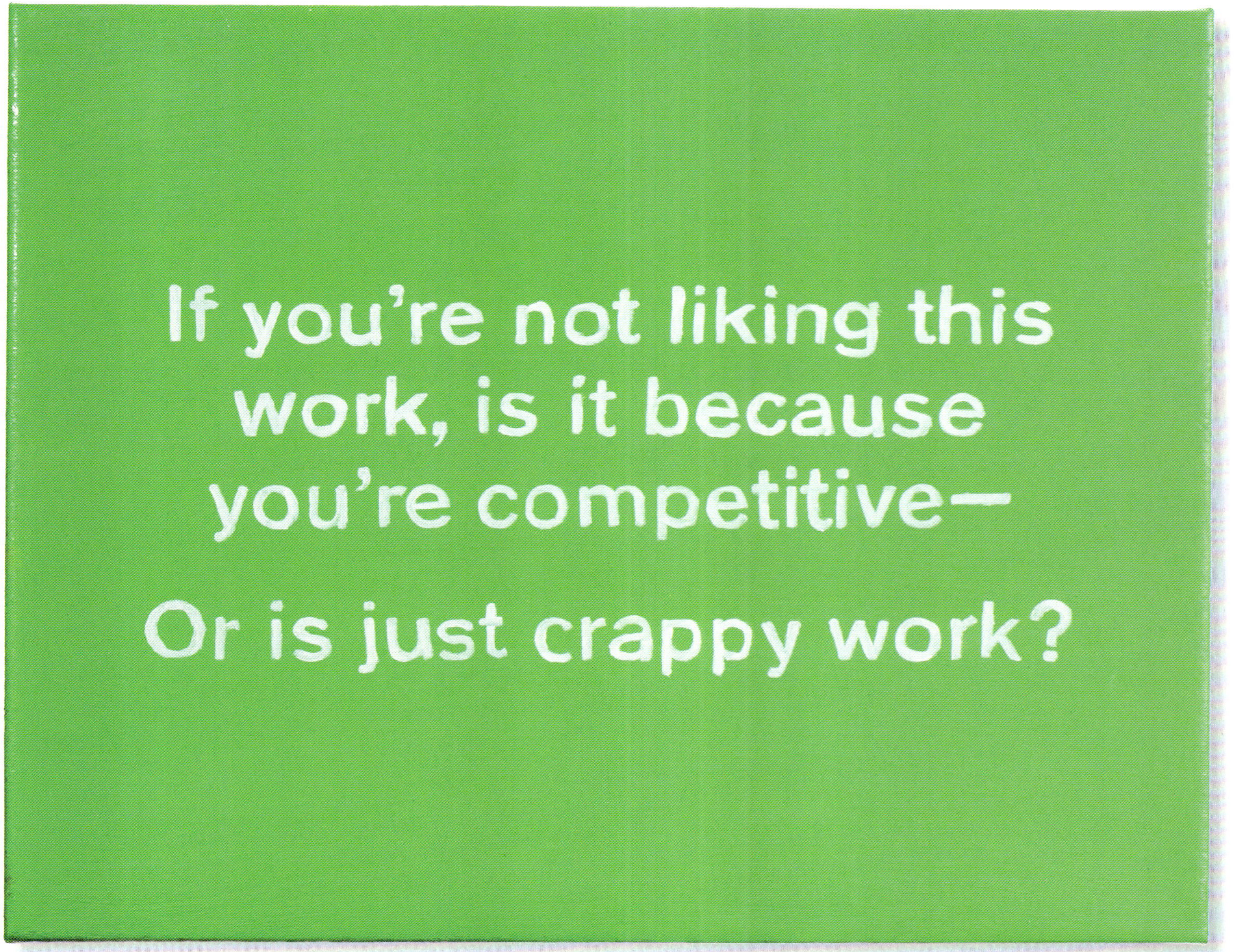

The Thoughts in My Head #14
2012
Acrylic on Canvas
11 x 14 inches

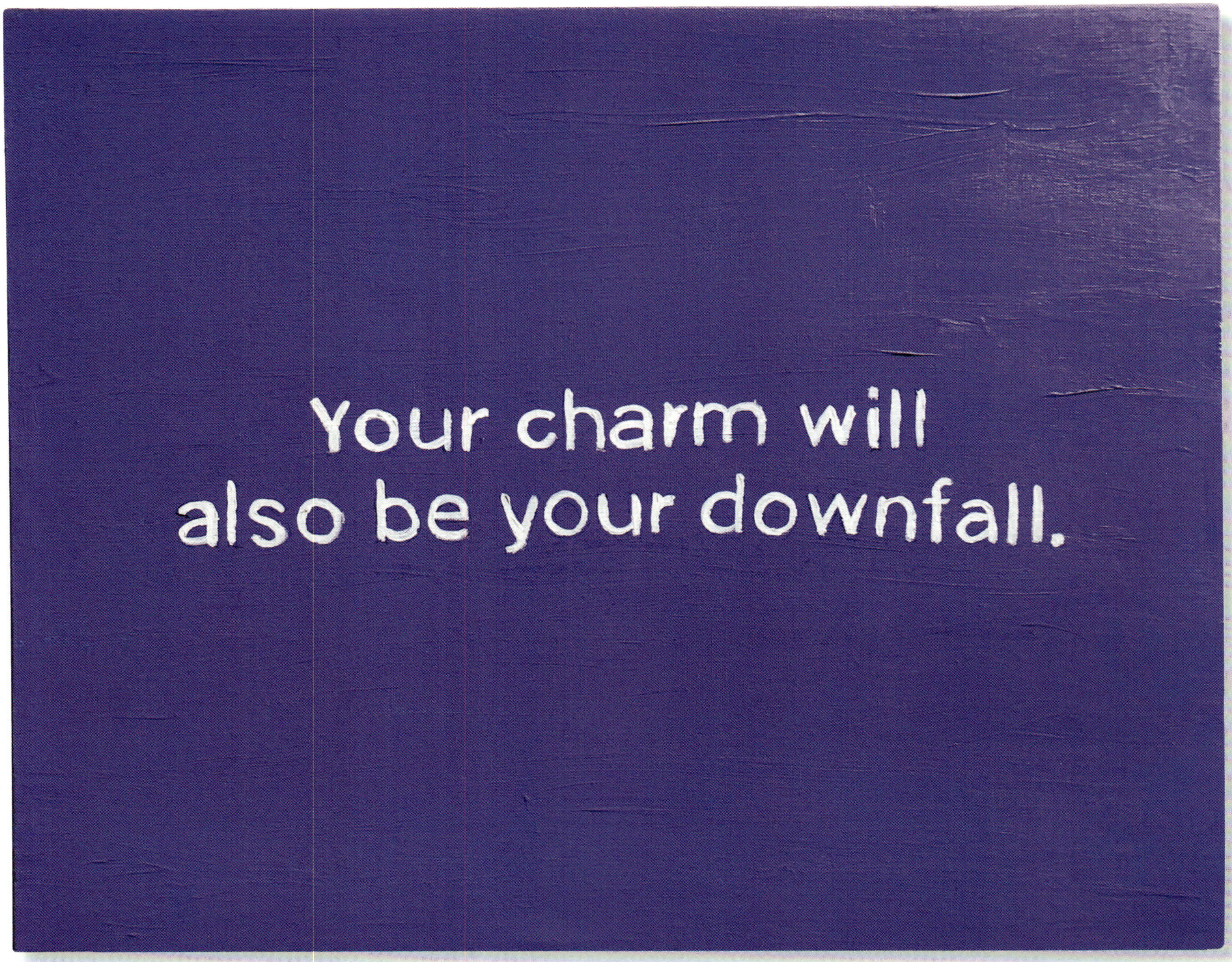

The Thoughts in My Head #15
2012
Acrylic on Canvas
11 x 14 inches

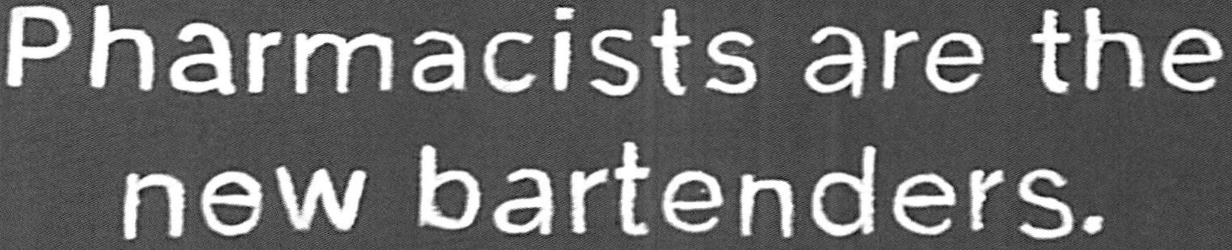

The Thoughts in My Head #16
2012
Acrylic on Canvas
11 x 14 inches

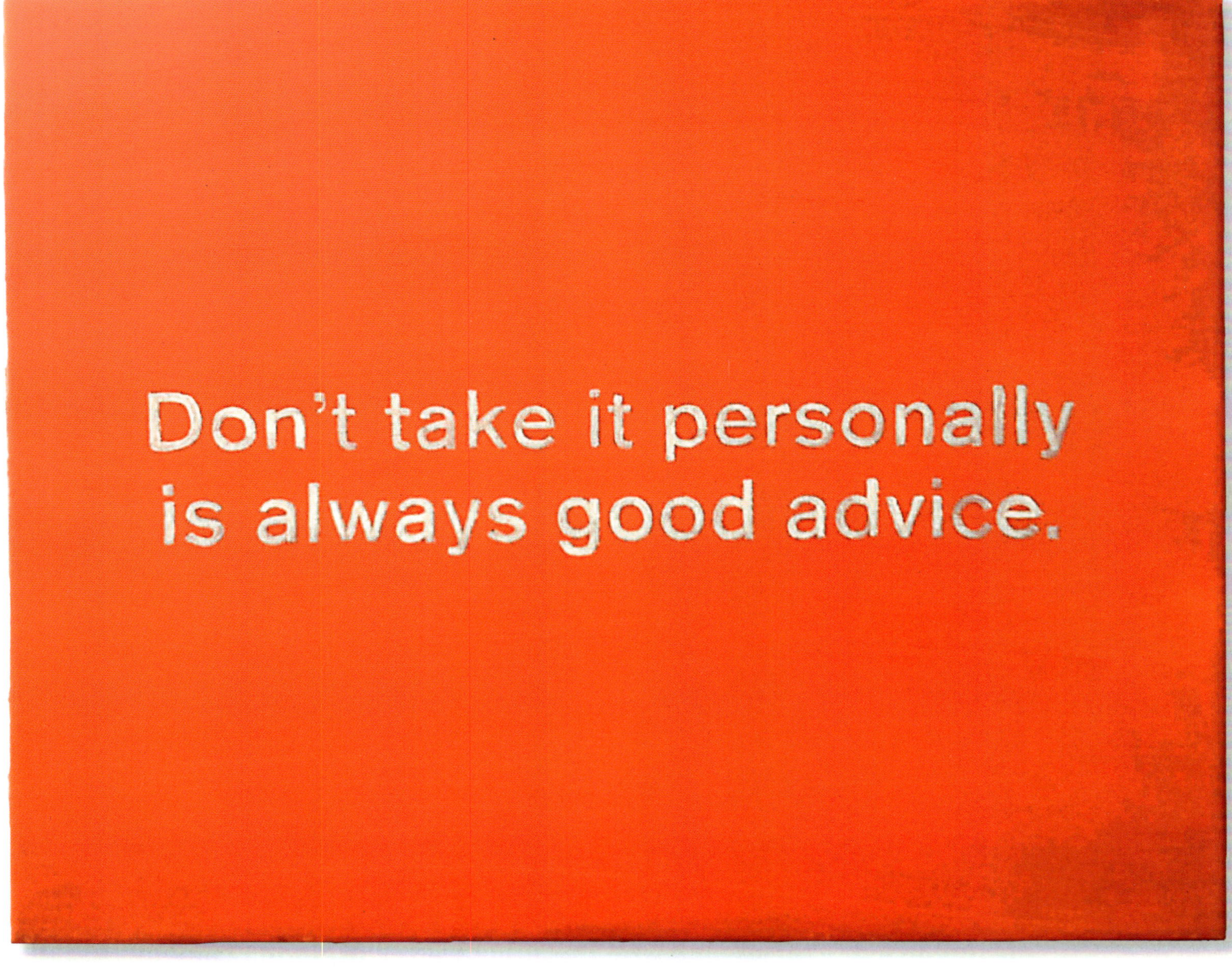

The Thoughts in My Head #17
2012
Acrylic on Canvas
11 x 14 inches

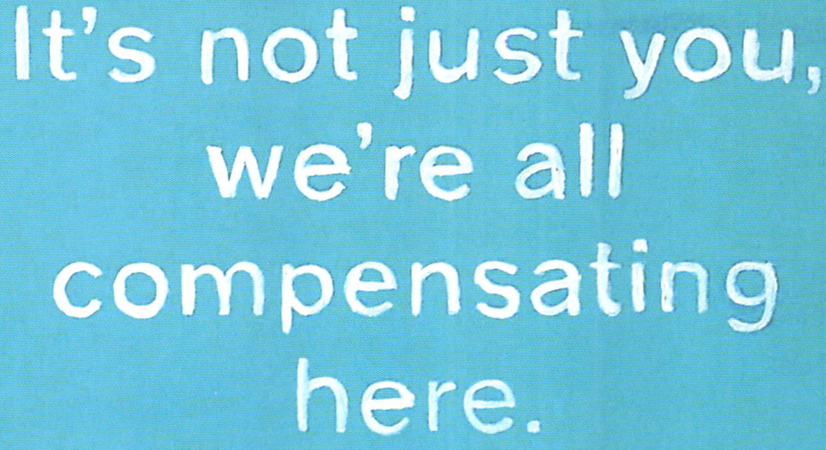

The Thoughts in My Head #18
2012
Acrylic on Canvas
11 x 14 inches

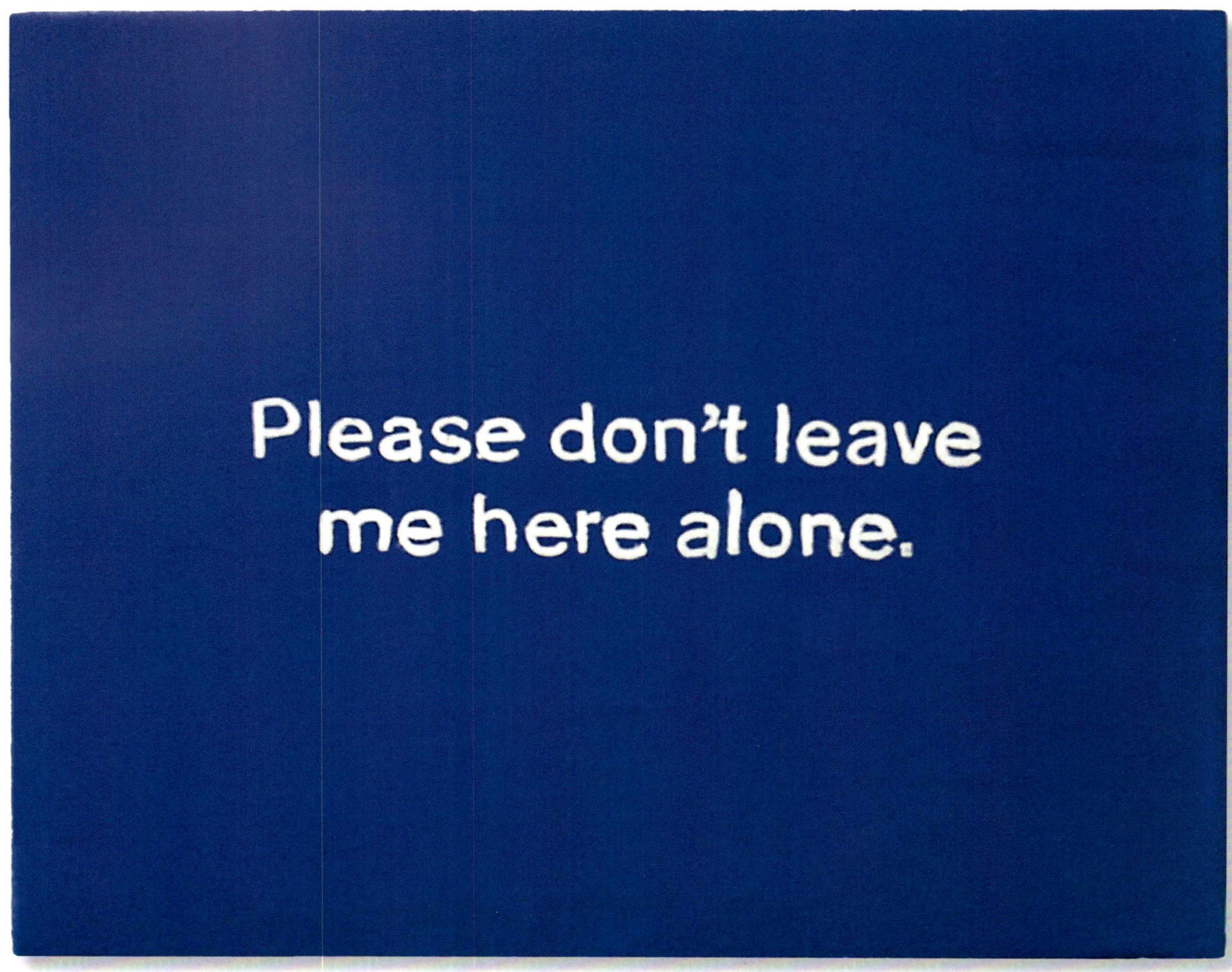

The Thoughts in My Head #19
2012
Acrylic on Canvas
11 x 14 inches

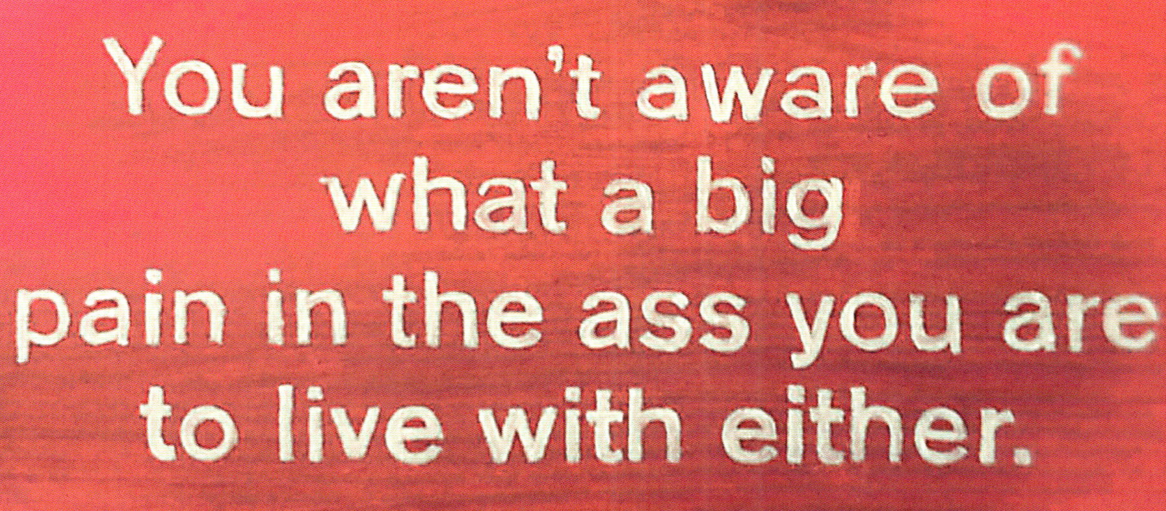

The Thoughts in My Head #20
2012
Acrylic on Canvas
11 x 14 inches

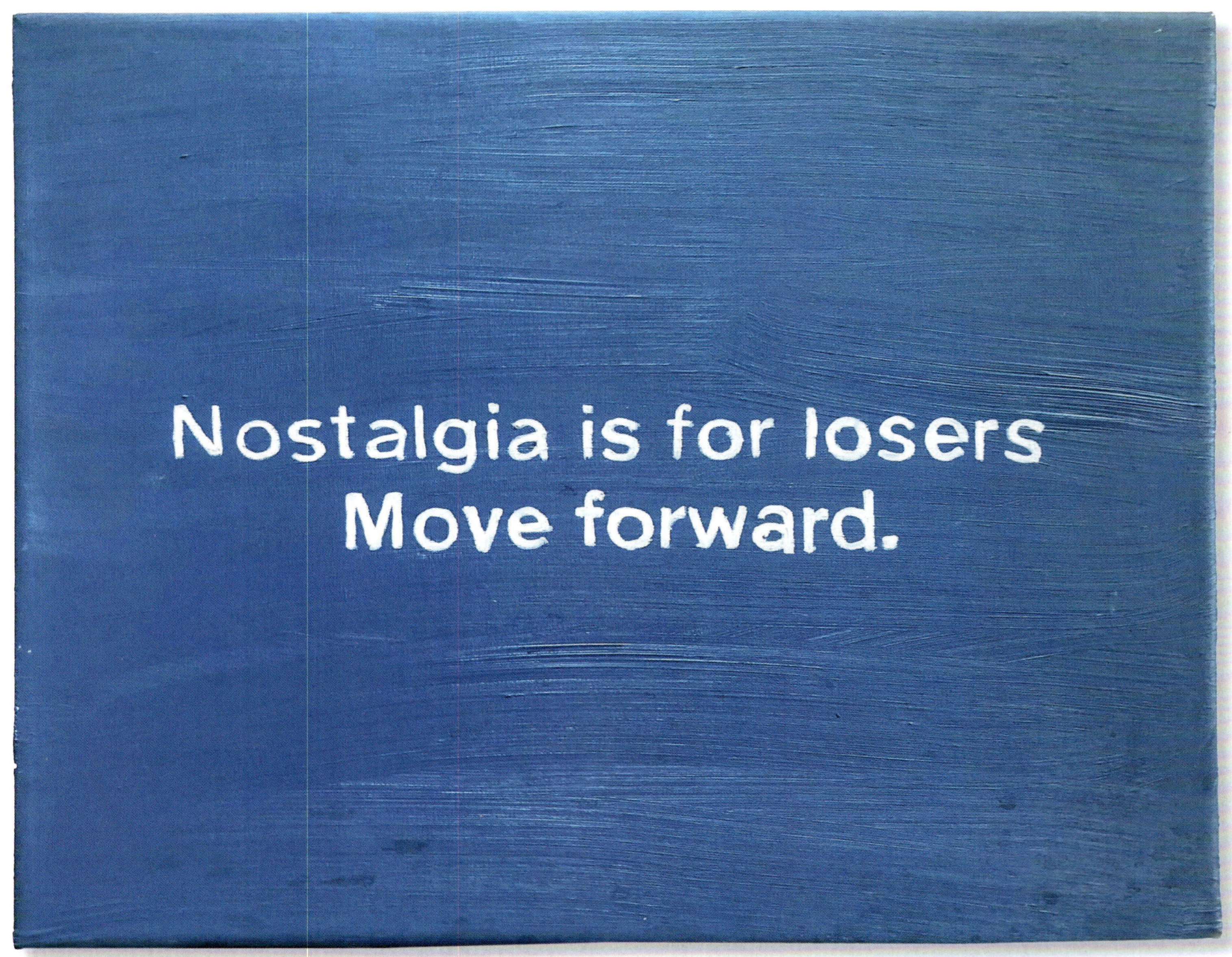

The Thoughts in My Head #21
2012
Acrylic on Canvas
11 x 14 inches

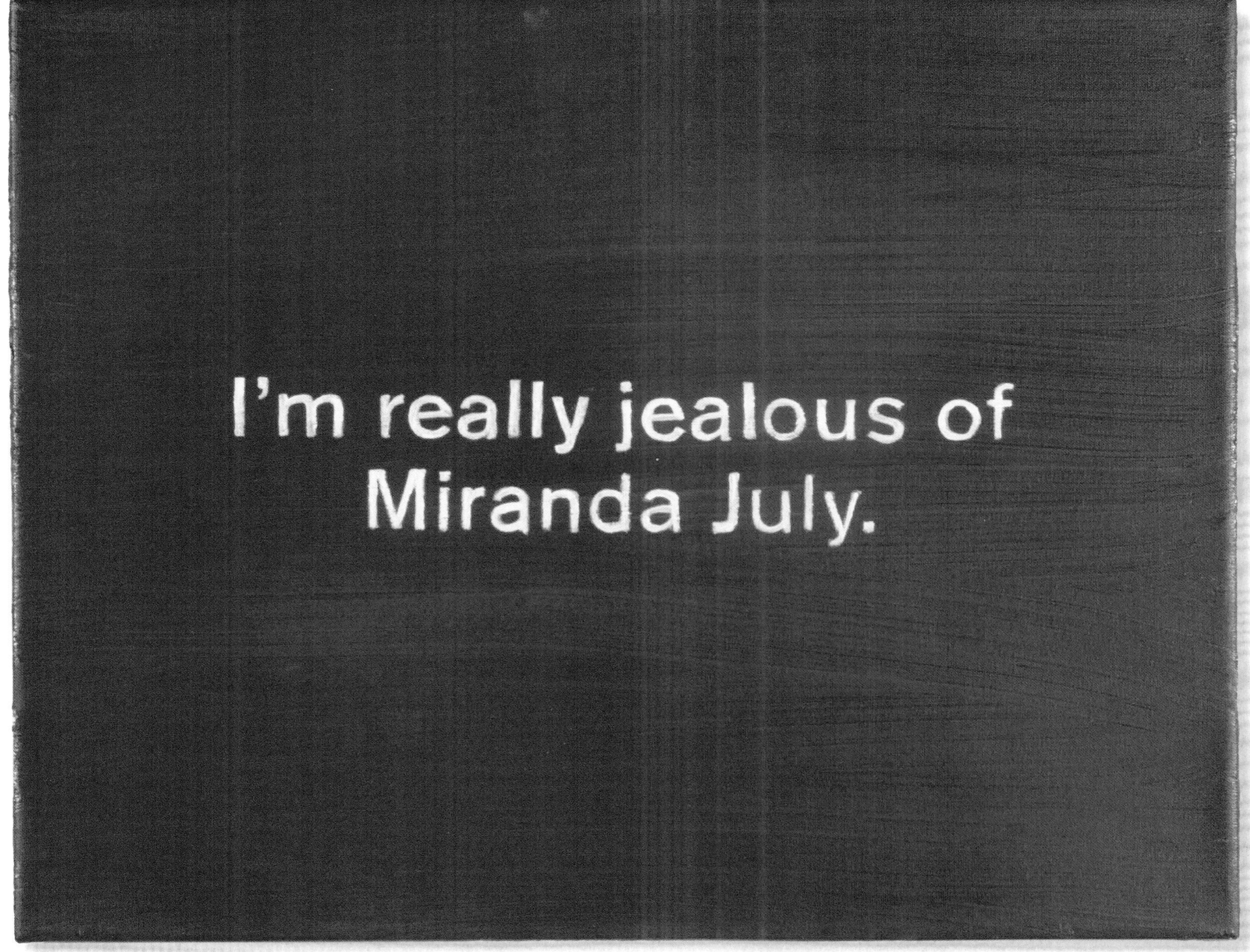

The Thoughts in My Head #22
2012
Acrylic on Canvas
11 x 14 inches

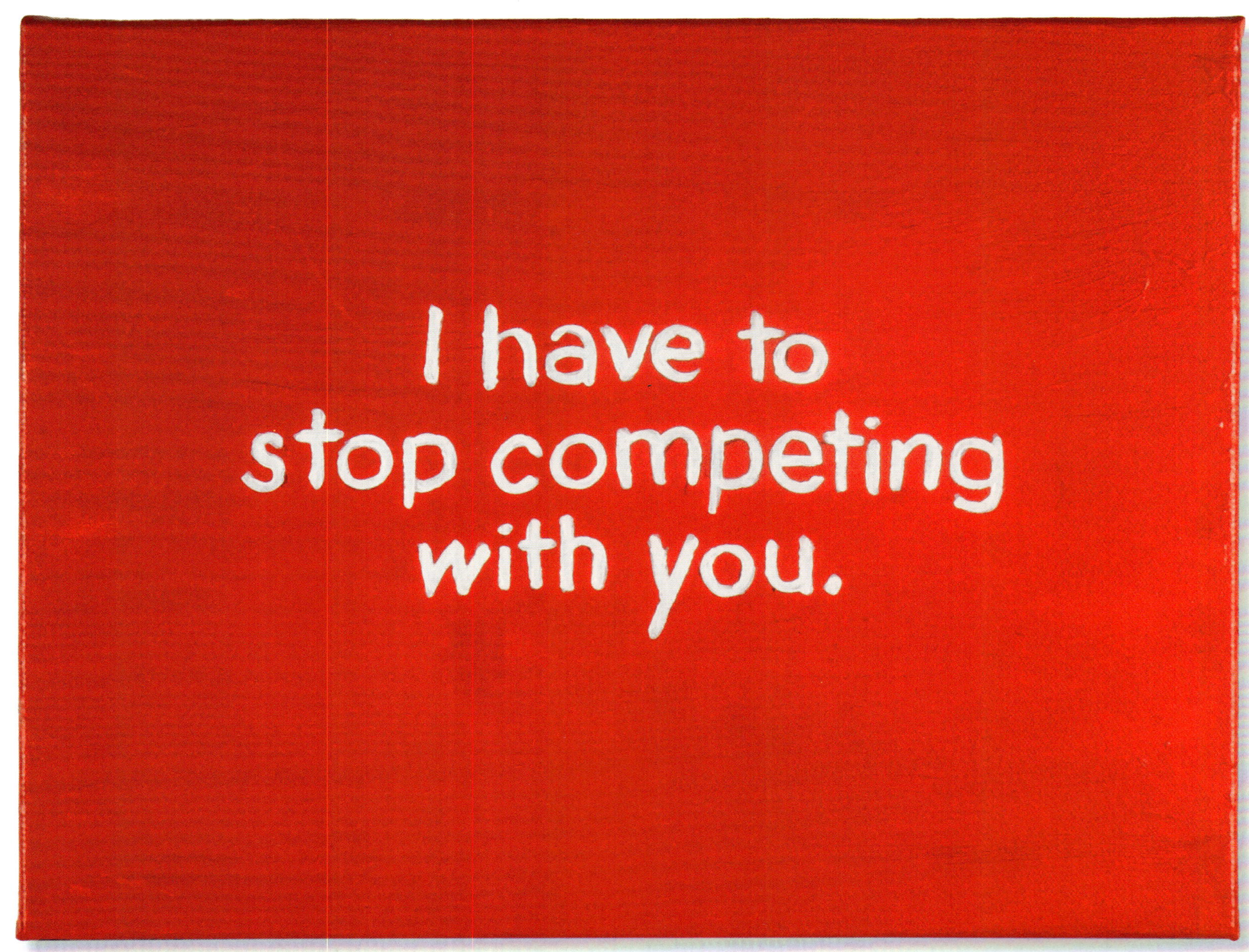

The Thoughts in My Head #23
2012
Acrylic on Canvas
11 x 14 inches

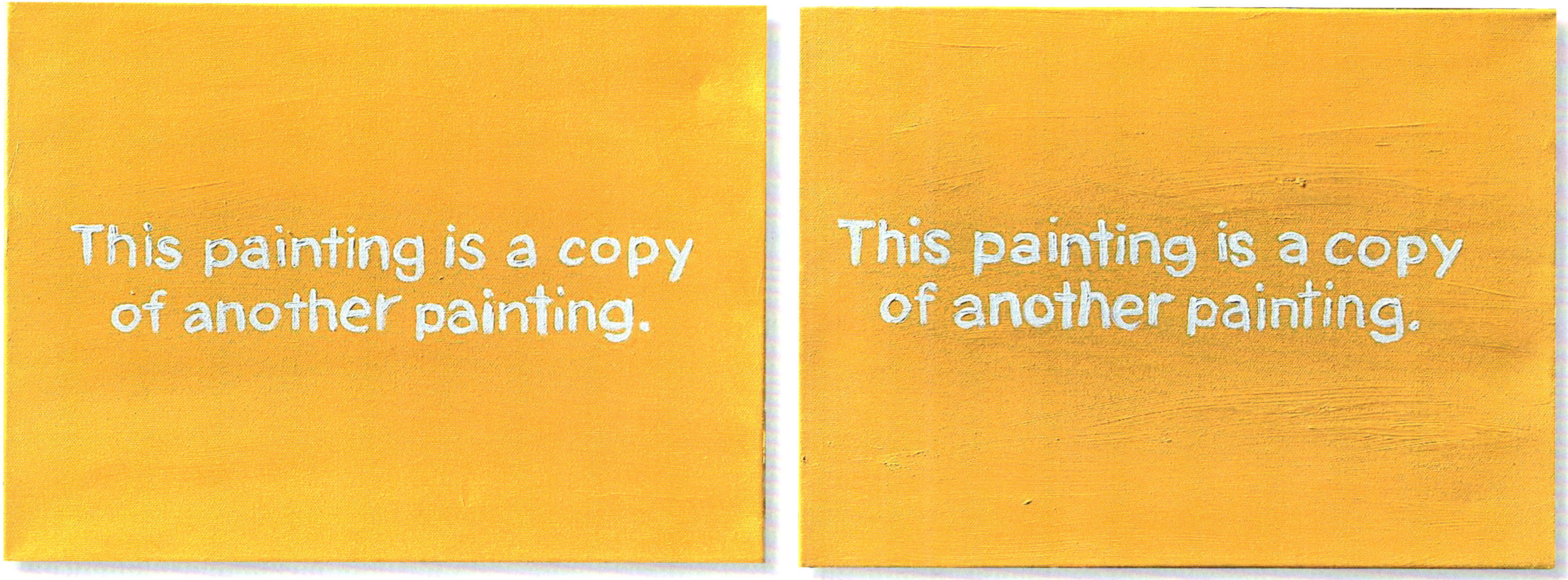

The Thoughts in My Head #24 (a+b)
2012
Acrylic on Canvas
11 x 14 inches

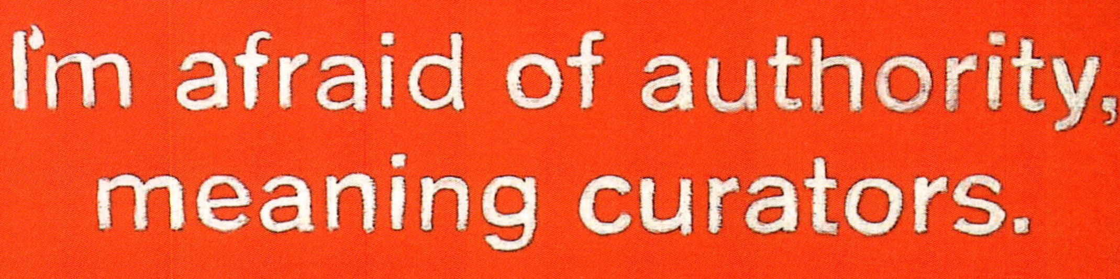

The Thoughts in My Head #25
2012
Acrylic on Canvas
11 x 14 inches

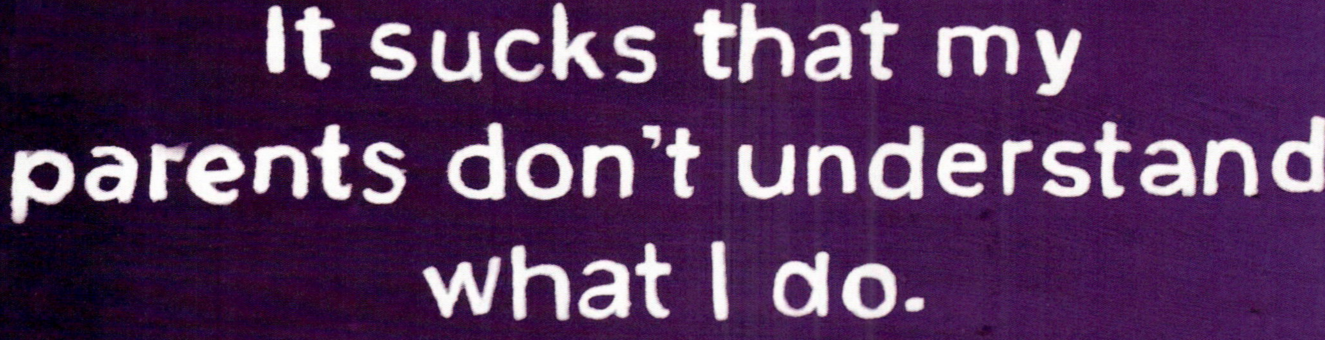

The Thoughts in My Head #26
2012
Acrylic on Canvas
11 x 14 inches

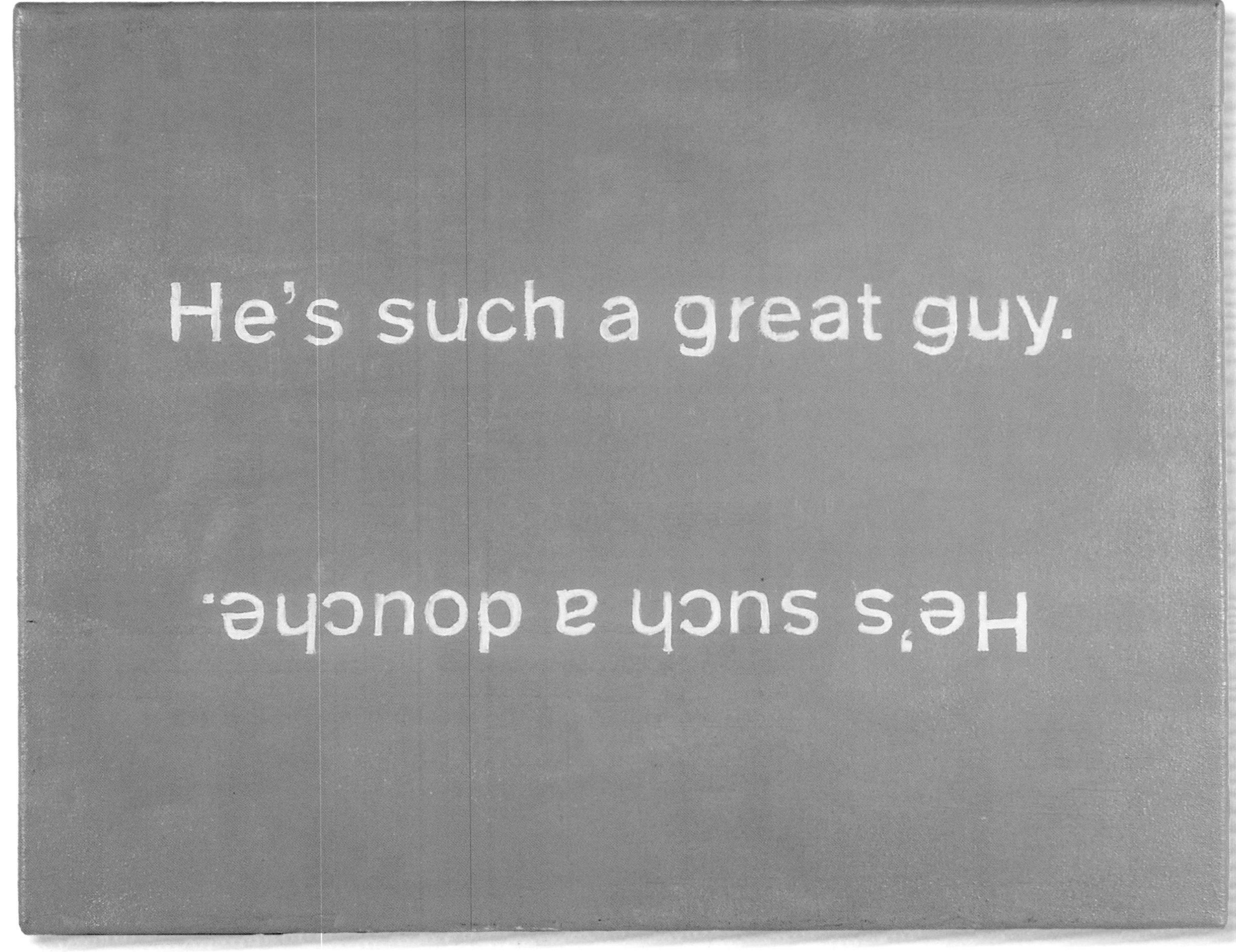

The Thoughts in My Head #27
2013
Acrylic on Canvas
11 x 14 inches

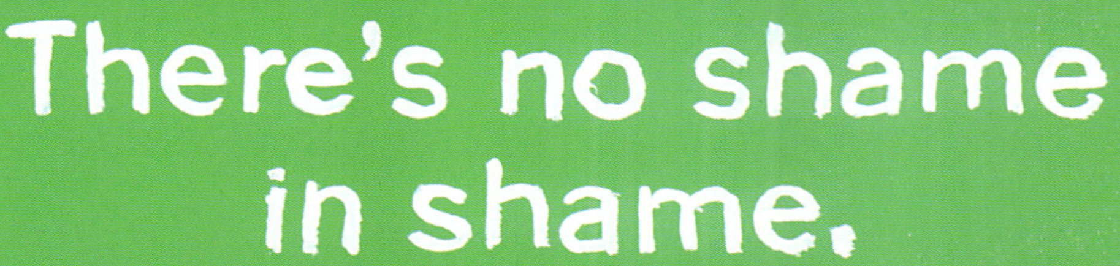

The Thoughts in My Head #28
2013
Acrylic on Canvas
11 x 14 inches

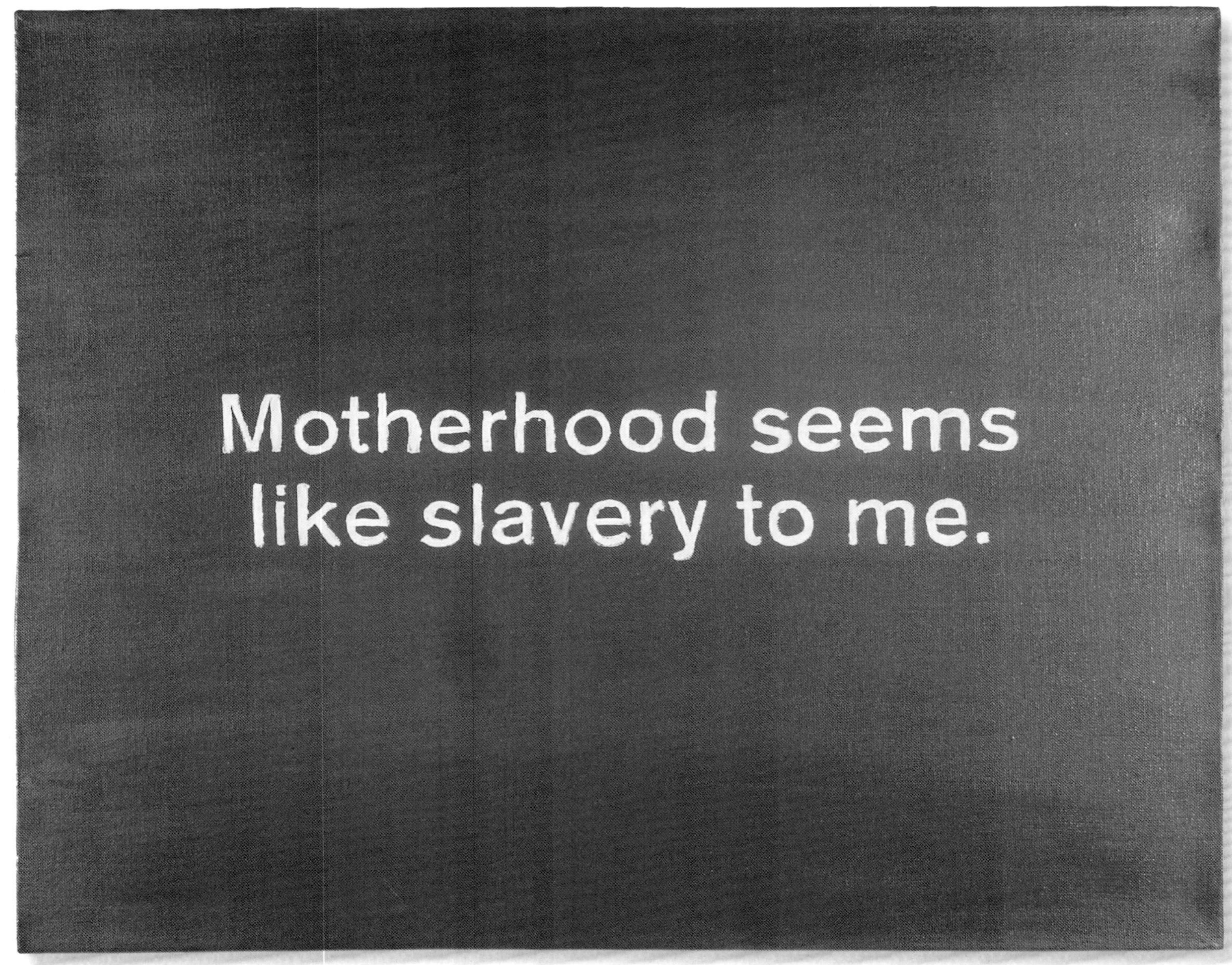

The Thoughts in My Head #29
2013
Acrylic on Canvas
11 x 14 inches

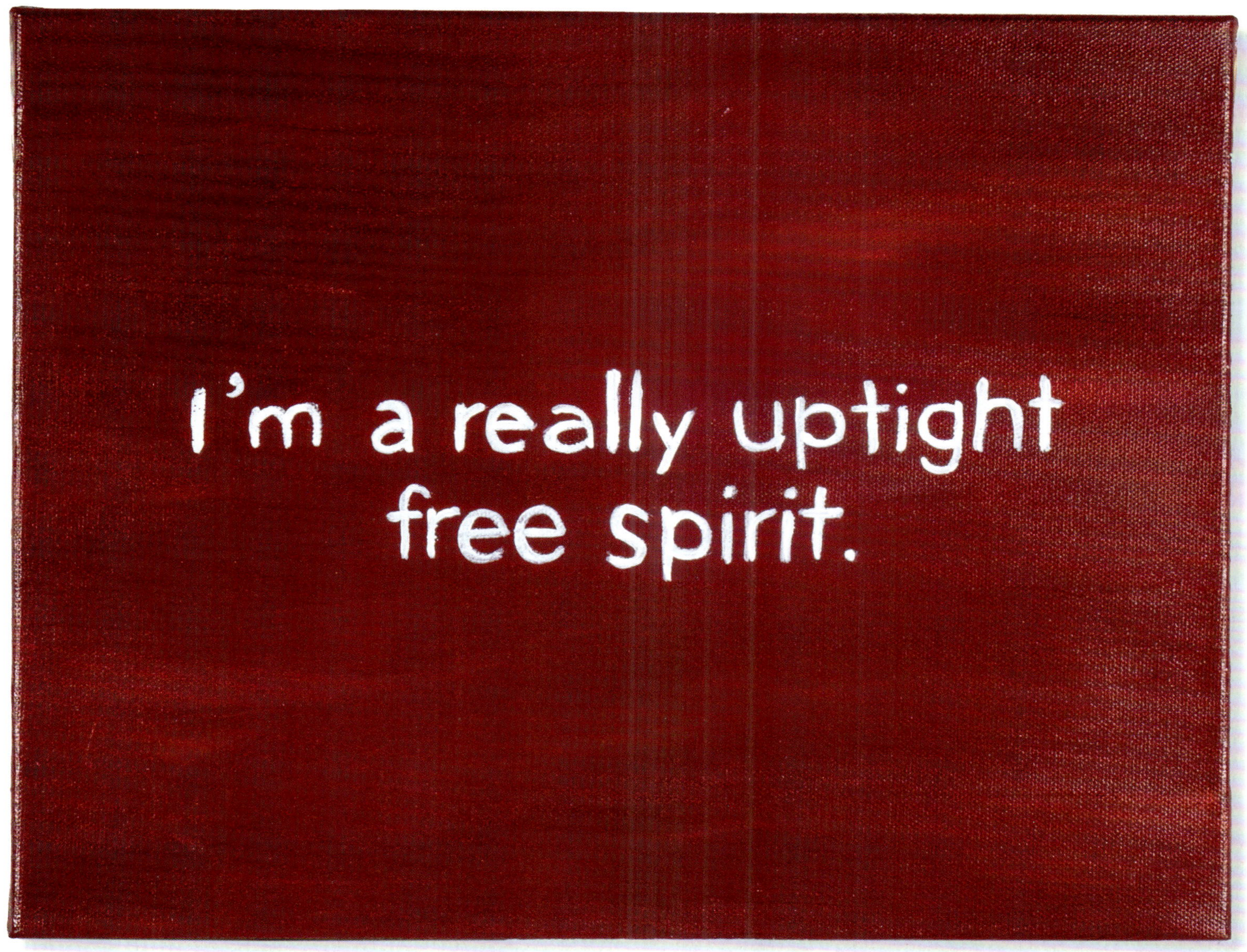

The Thoughts in My Head #30
2013
Acrylic on Canvas
11 x 14 inches

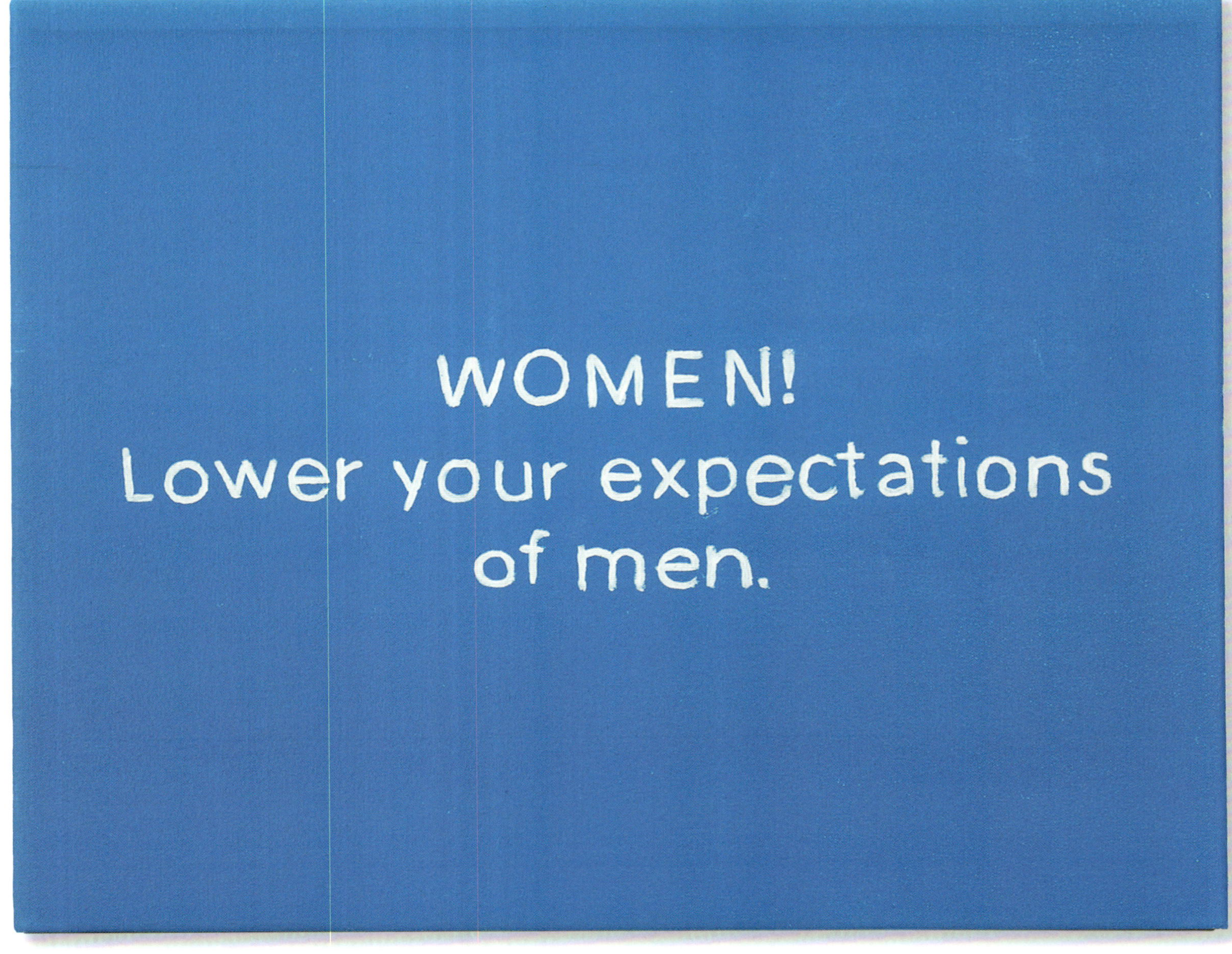

The Thoughts in My Head #31
2013
Acrylic on Canvas
11 x 14 inches

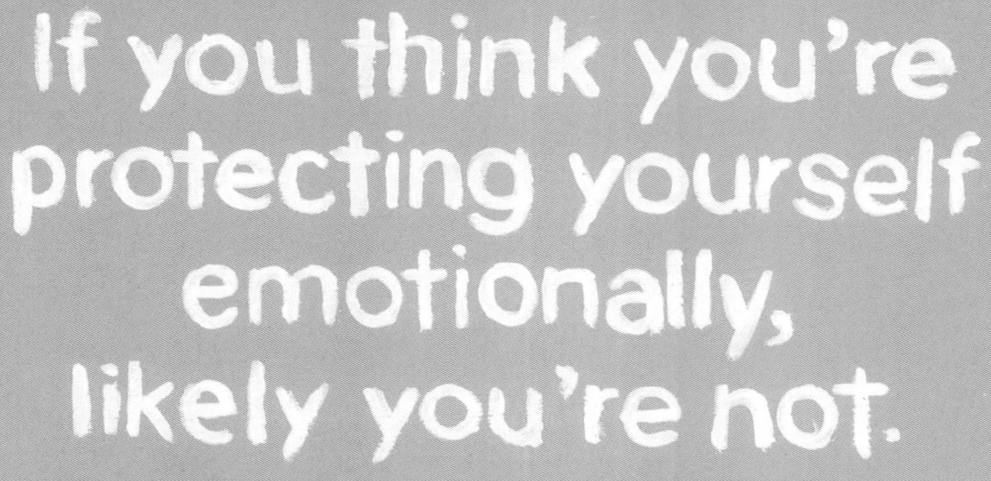

The Thoughts in My Head #32
2013
Acrylic on Canvas
11 x 14 inches

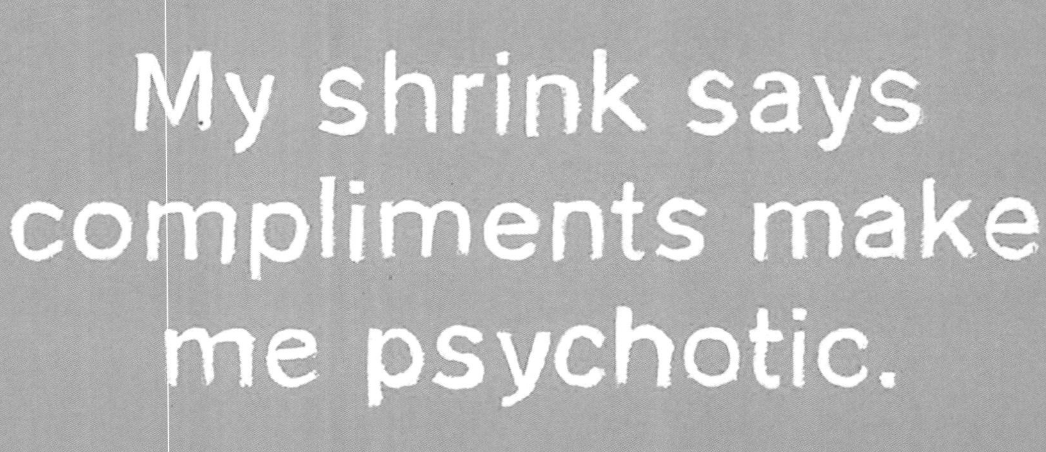

The Thoughts in My Head #33
2013
Acrylic on Canvas
11 x 14 inches

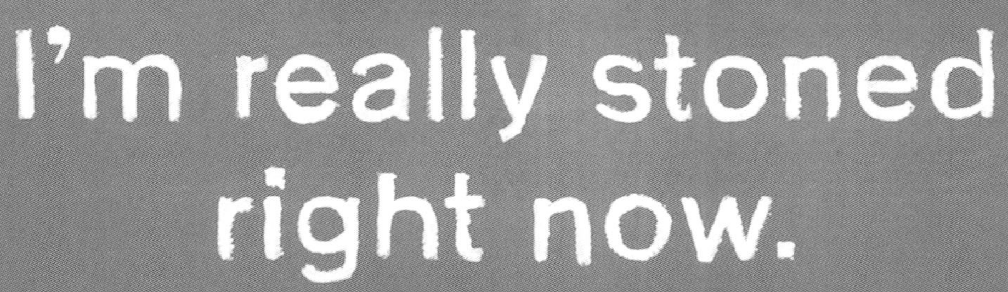

The Thoughts in My Head #34
2013
Acrylic on Canvas
11 x 14 inches

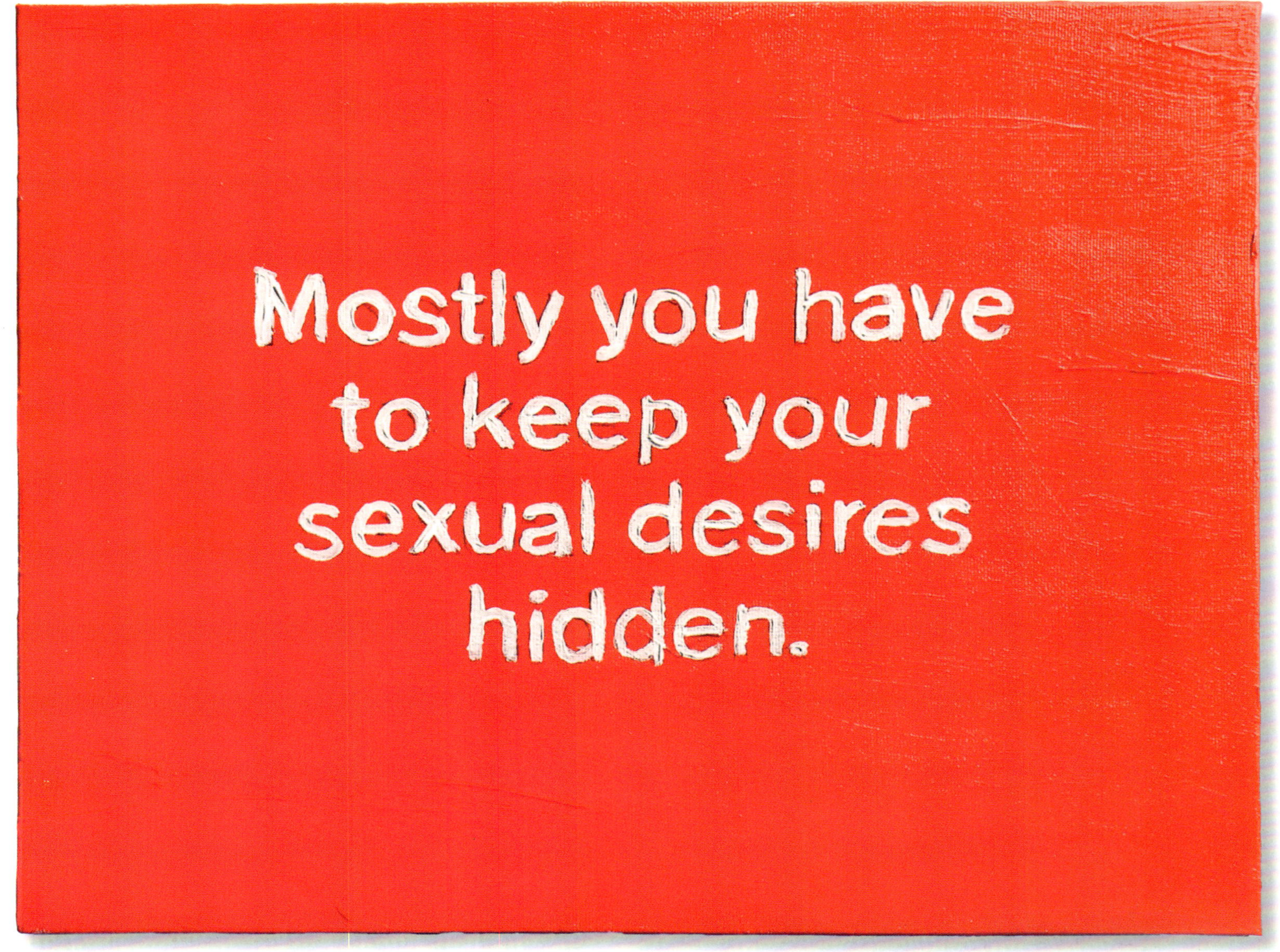

The Thoughts in My Head #35
2013
Acrylic on Canvas
11 x 14 inches

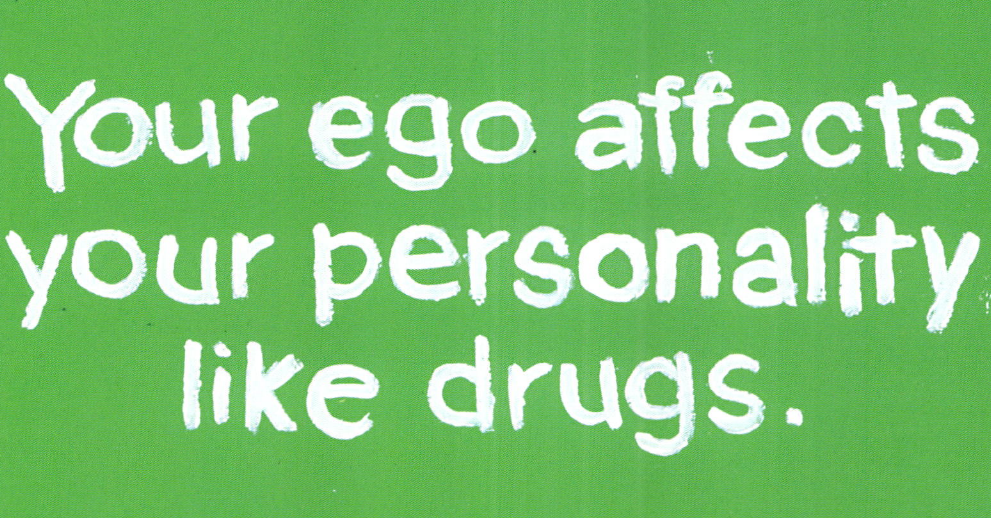

The Thoughts in My Head #36
2013
Acrylic on Canvas
11 x 14 inches

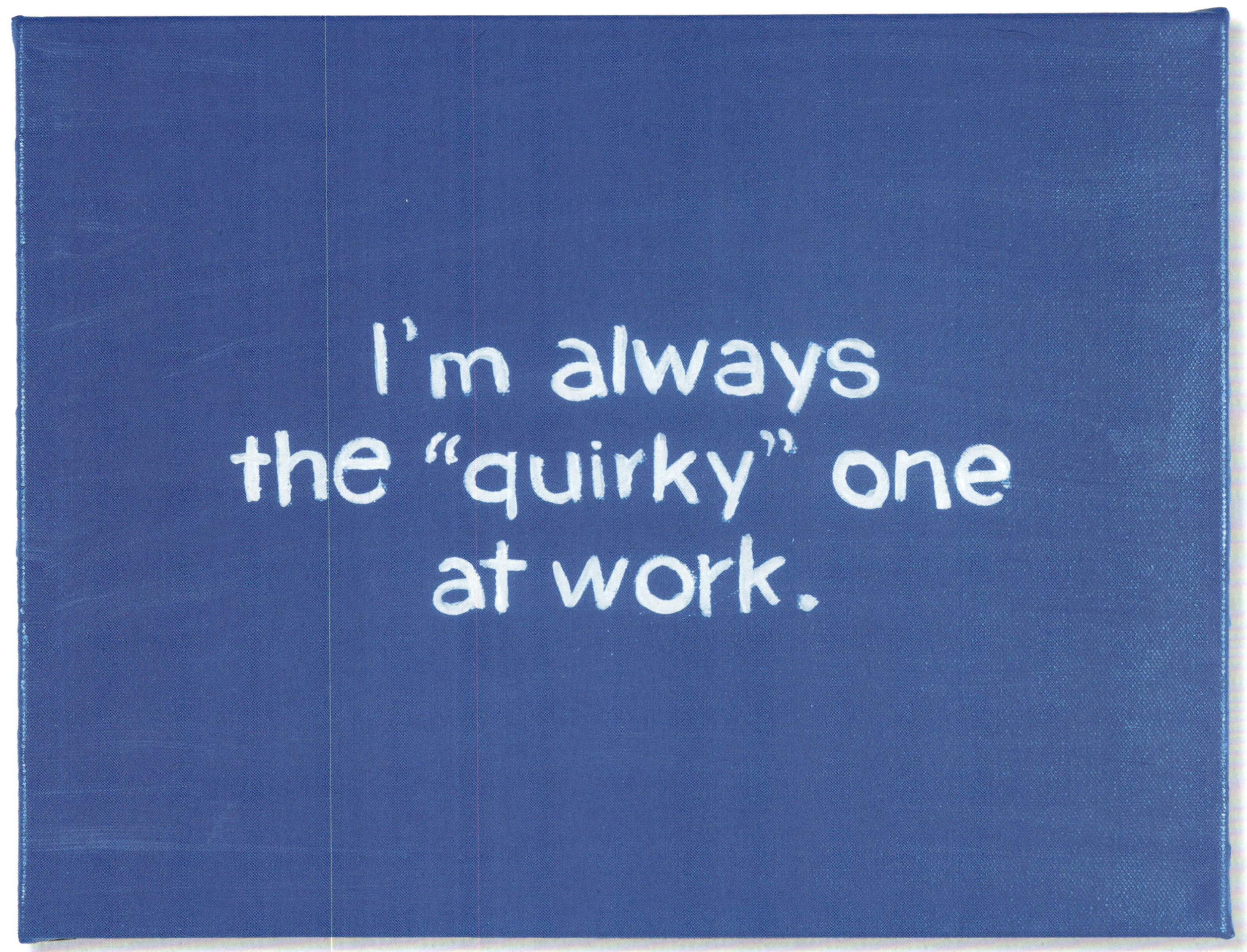

The Thoughts in My Head #37
2013
Acrylic on Canvas
11 x 14 inches

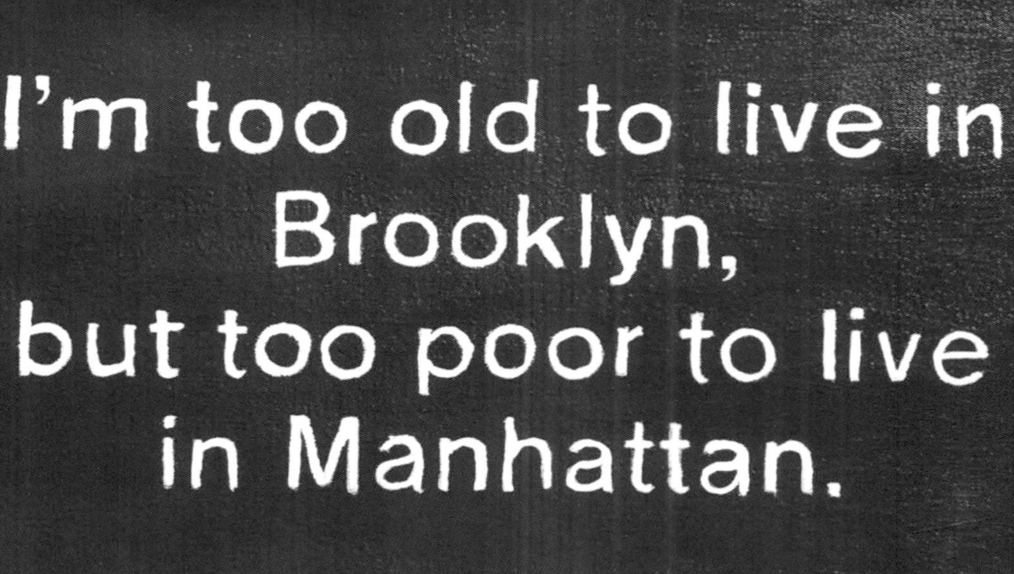

The Thoughts in My Head #38
2013
Acrylic on Canvas
11 x 14 inches

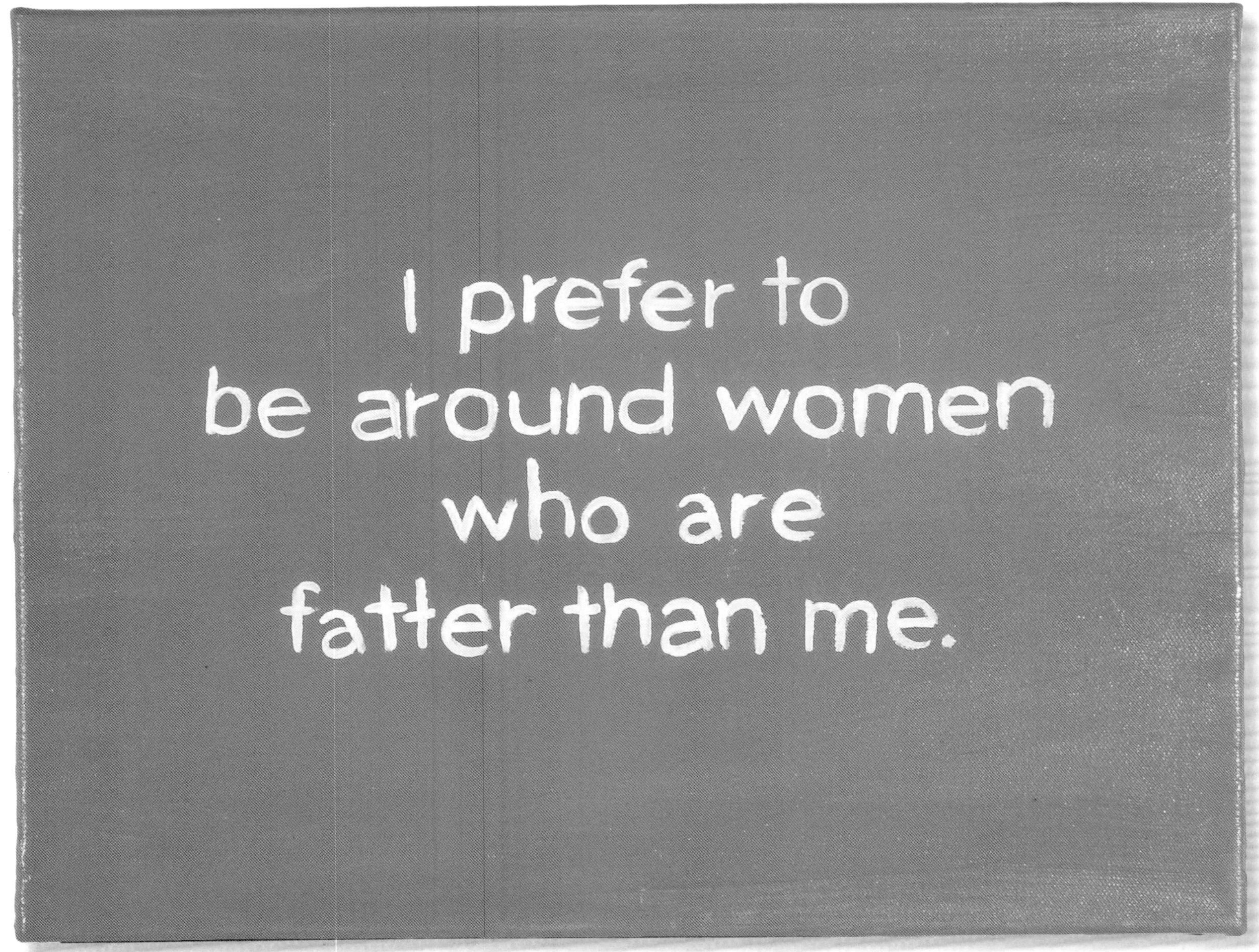

The Thoughts in My Head #39
2013
Acrylic on Canvas
11 x 14 inches

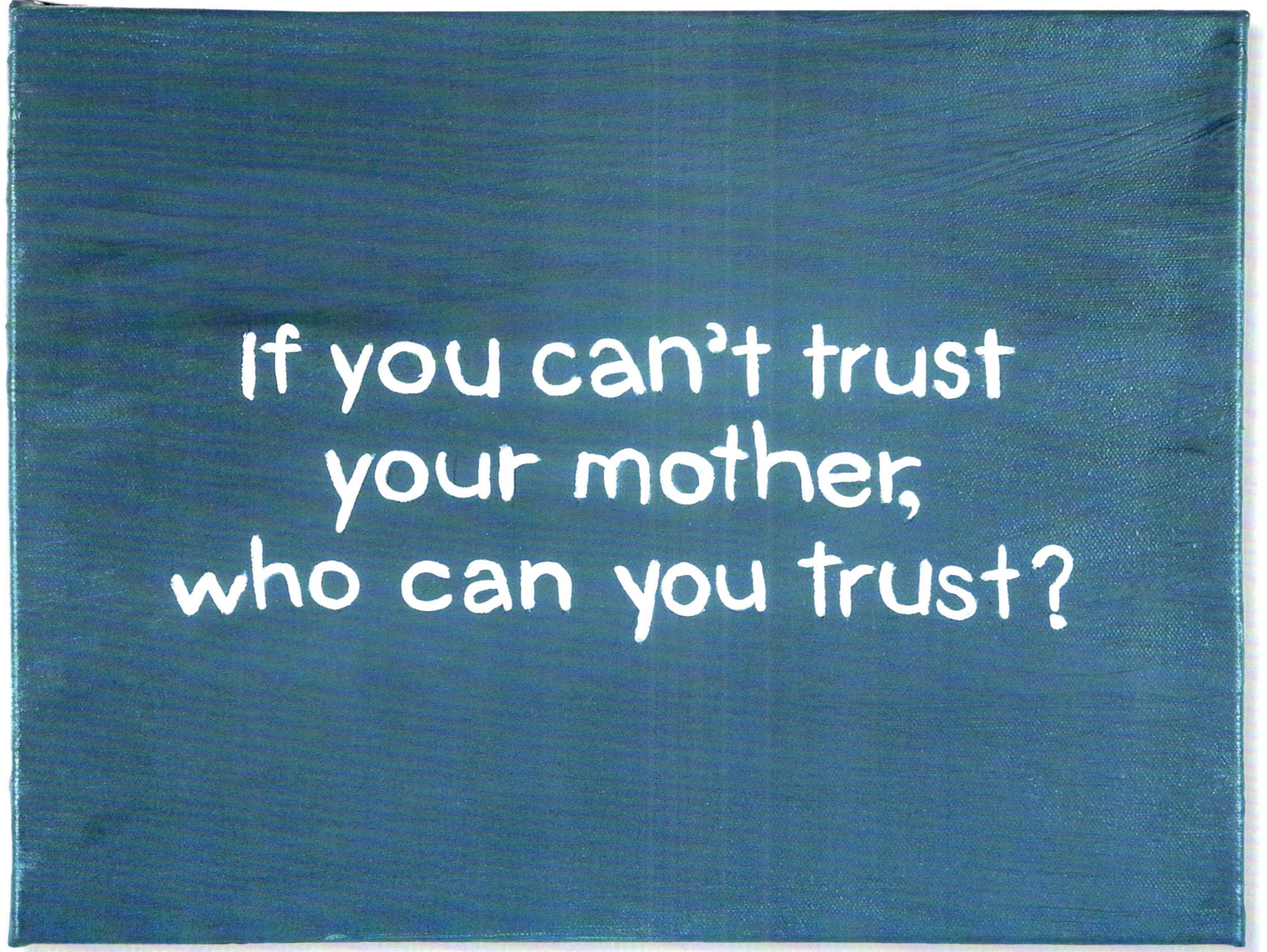

The Thoughts in My Head #40
2013
Acrylic on Canvas
11 x 14 inches

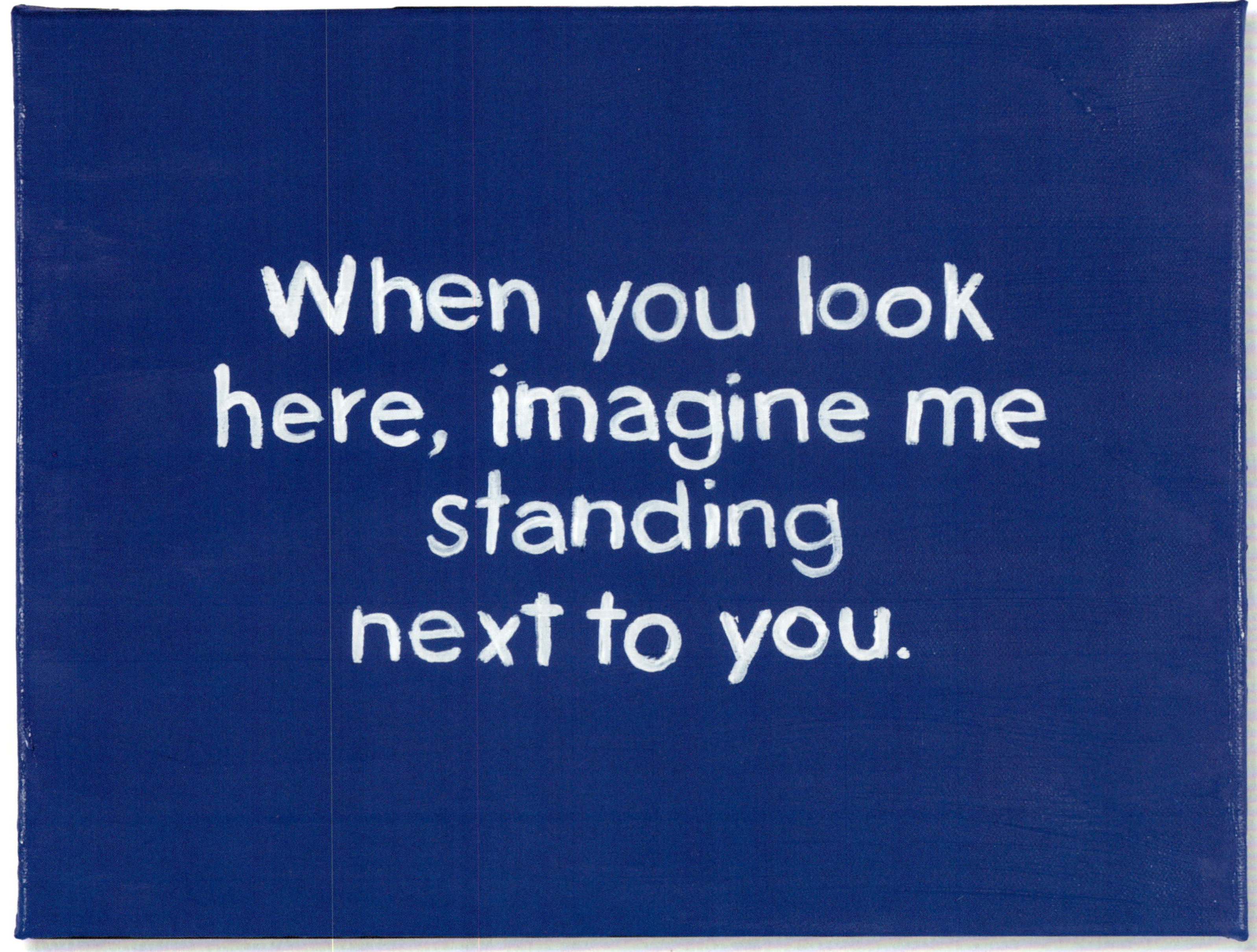

The Thoughts in My Head #41
2013
Acrylic on Canvas
11 x 14 inches

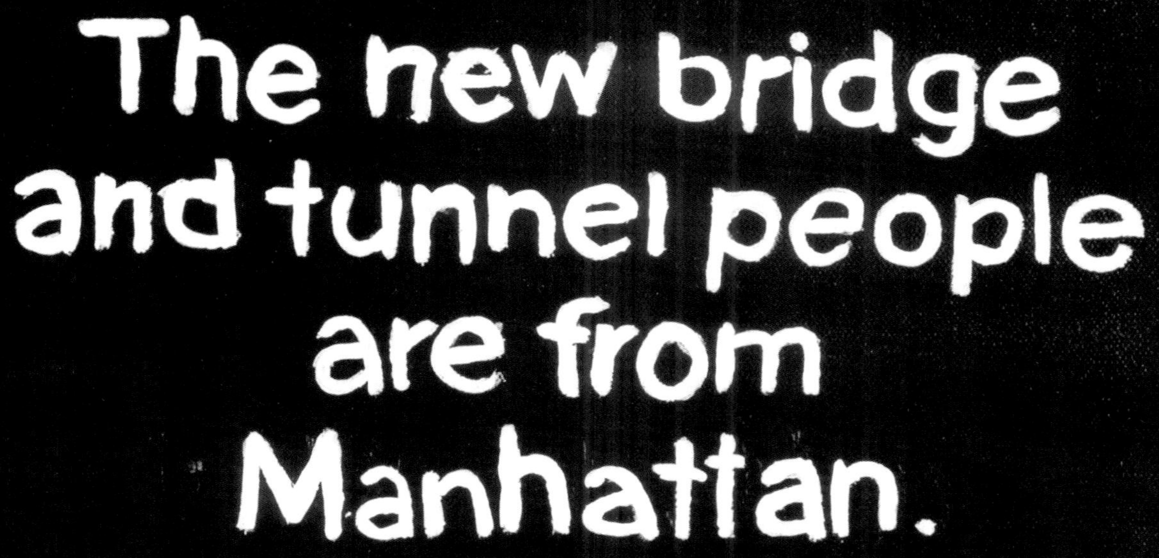

The Thoughts in My Head #42
2013
Acrylic on Canvas
11 x 14 inches

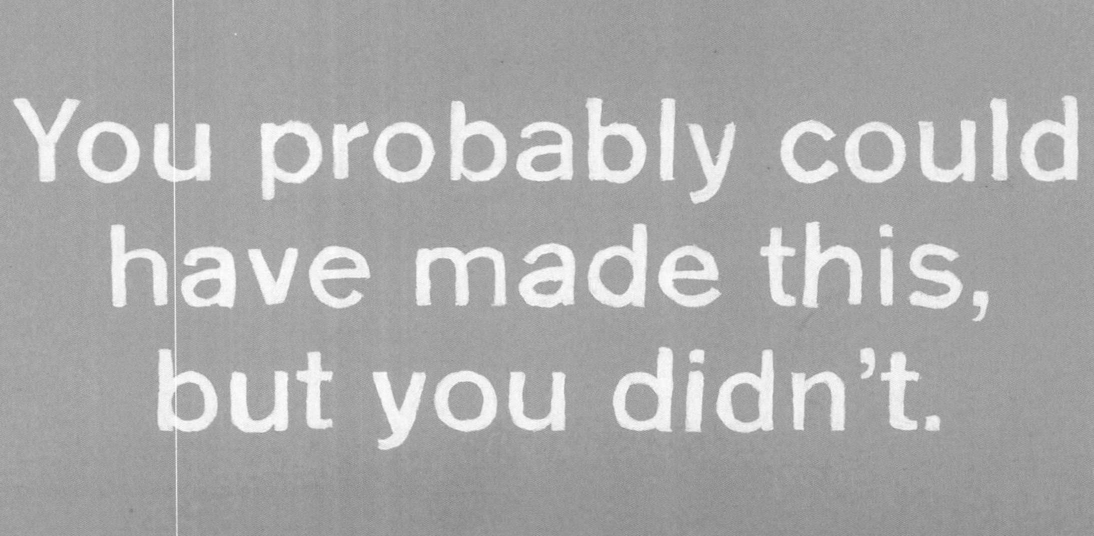

The Thoughts in My Head #43
2014
Acrylic on Canvas
11 x 14 inches

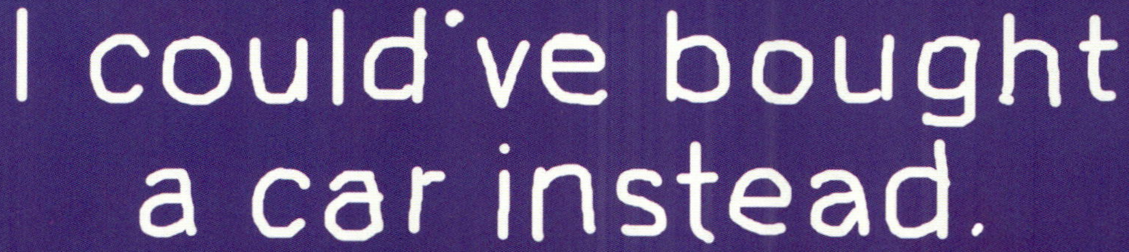

The Thoughts in My Head #44
2014
Acrylic on Canvas
11 x 14 inches

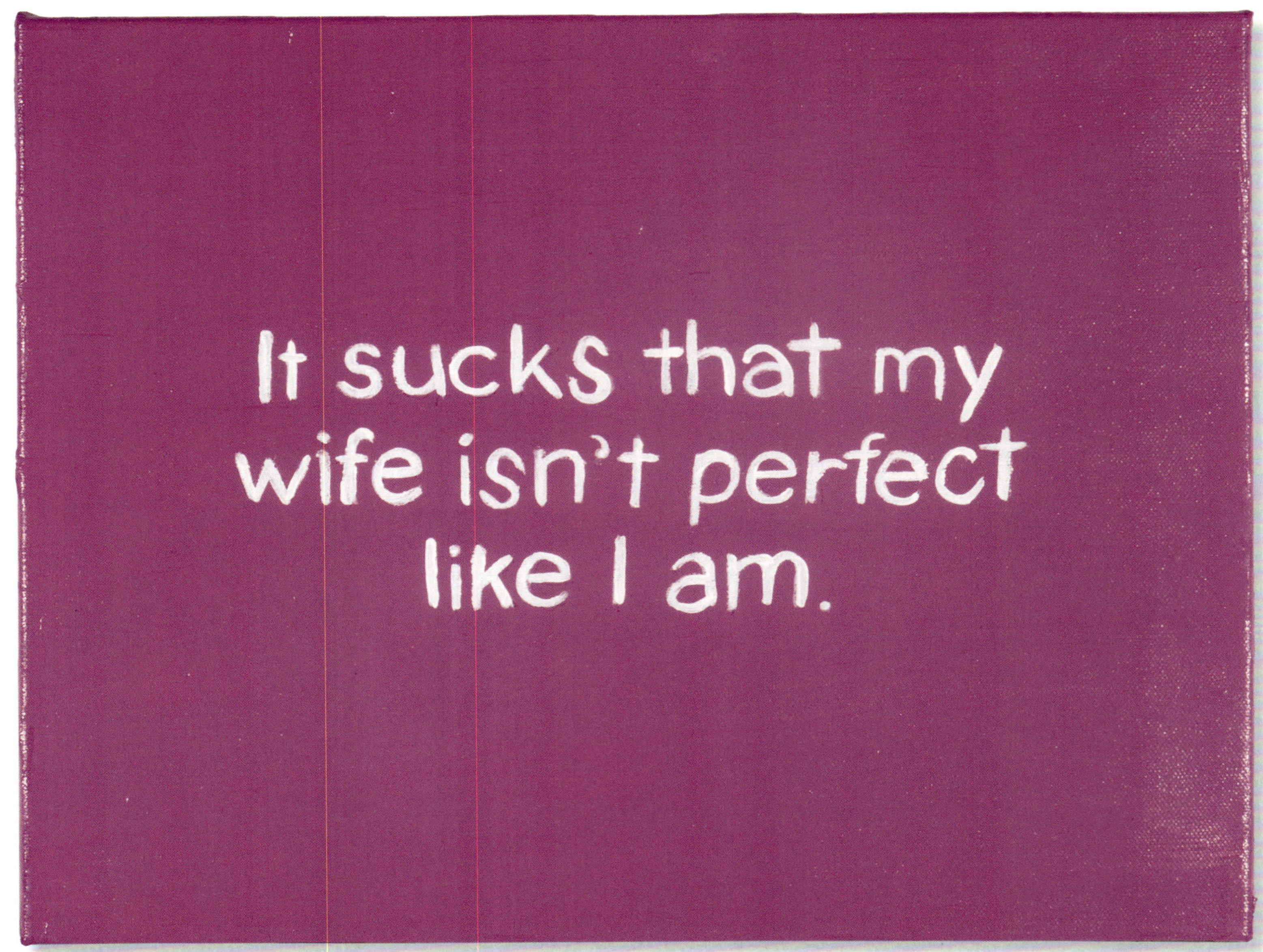

The Thoughts in My Head #45
2014
Acrylic on Canvas
11 x 14 inches

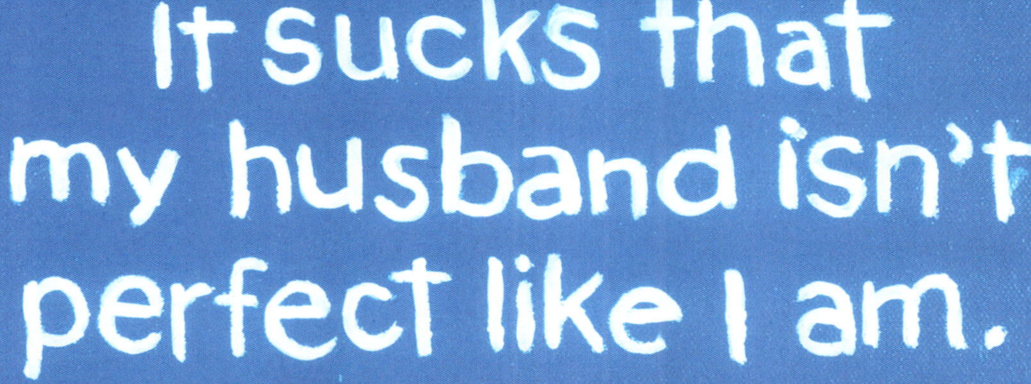

The Thoughts in My Head #46
2014
Acrylic on Canvas
11 x 14 inches

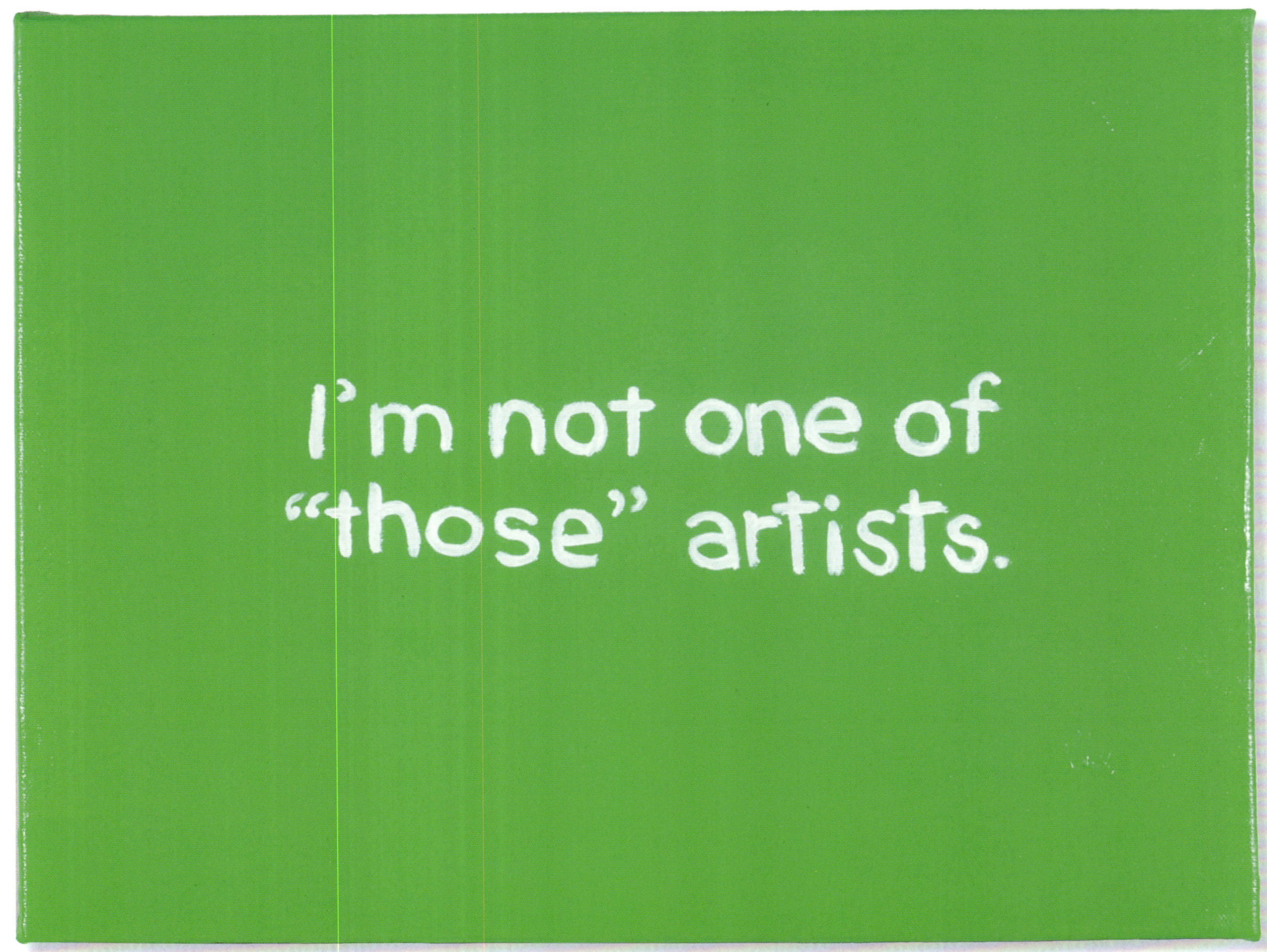

The Thoughts in My Head #47
2014
Acrylic on Canvas
11 x 14 inches

The Thoughts in My Head #48
2014
Acrylic on Canvas
11 x 14 inches

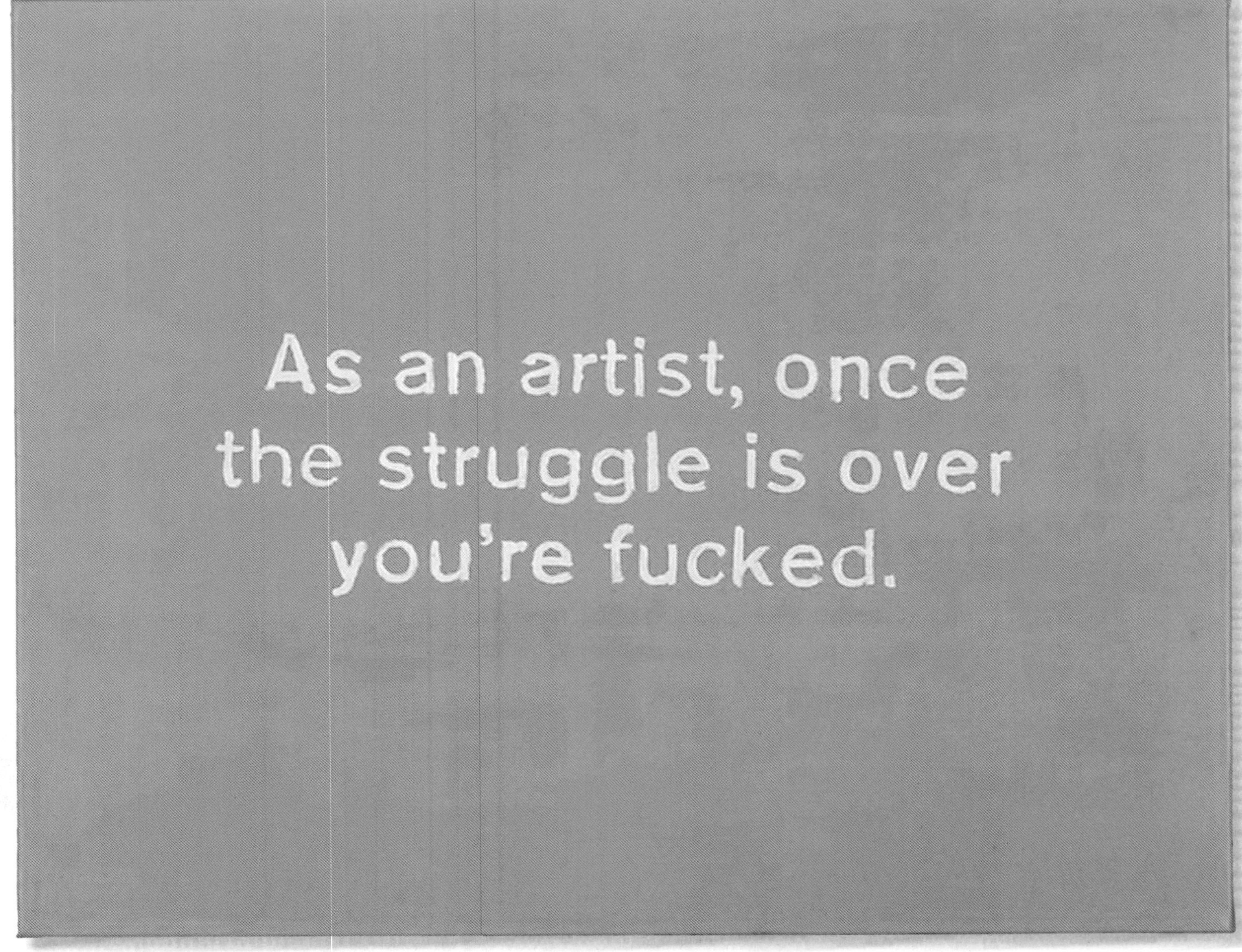

The Thoughts in My Head #49
2014
Acrylic on Canvas
11 x 14 inches

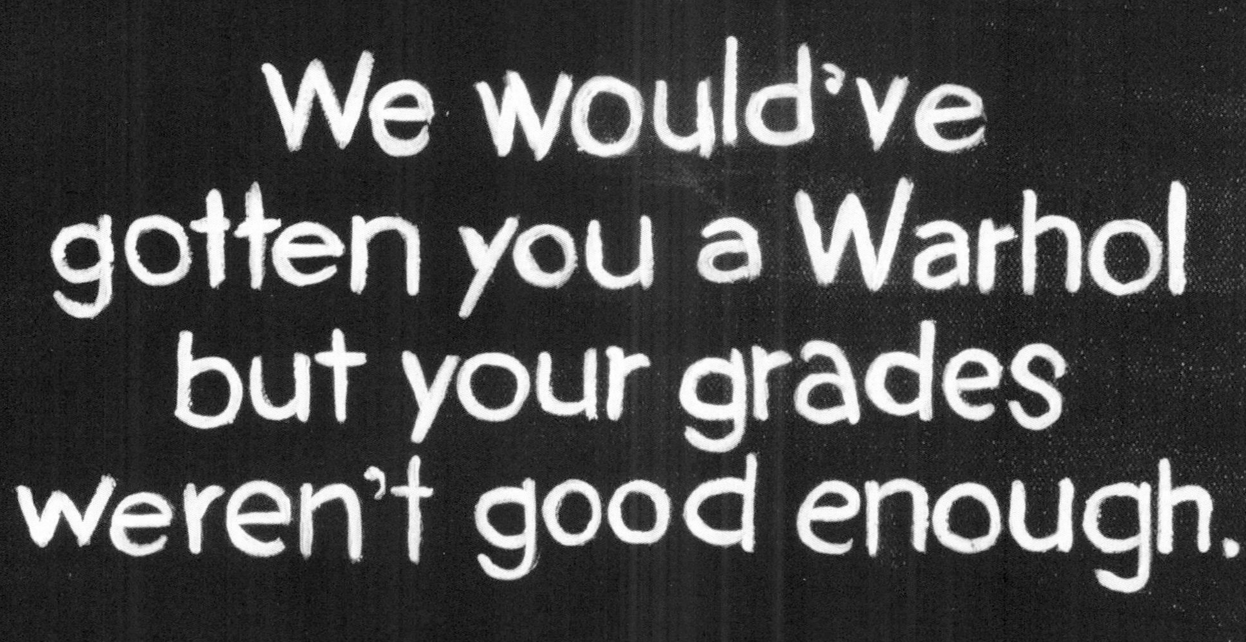

The Thoughts in My Head #50
2014
Acrylic on Canvas
11 x 14 inches

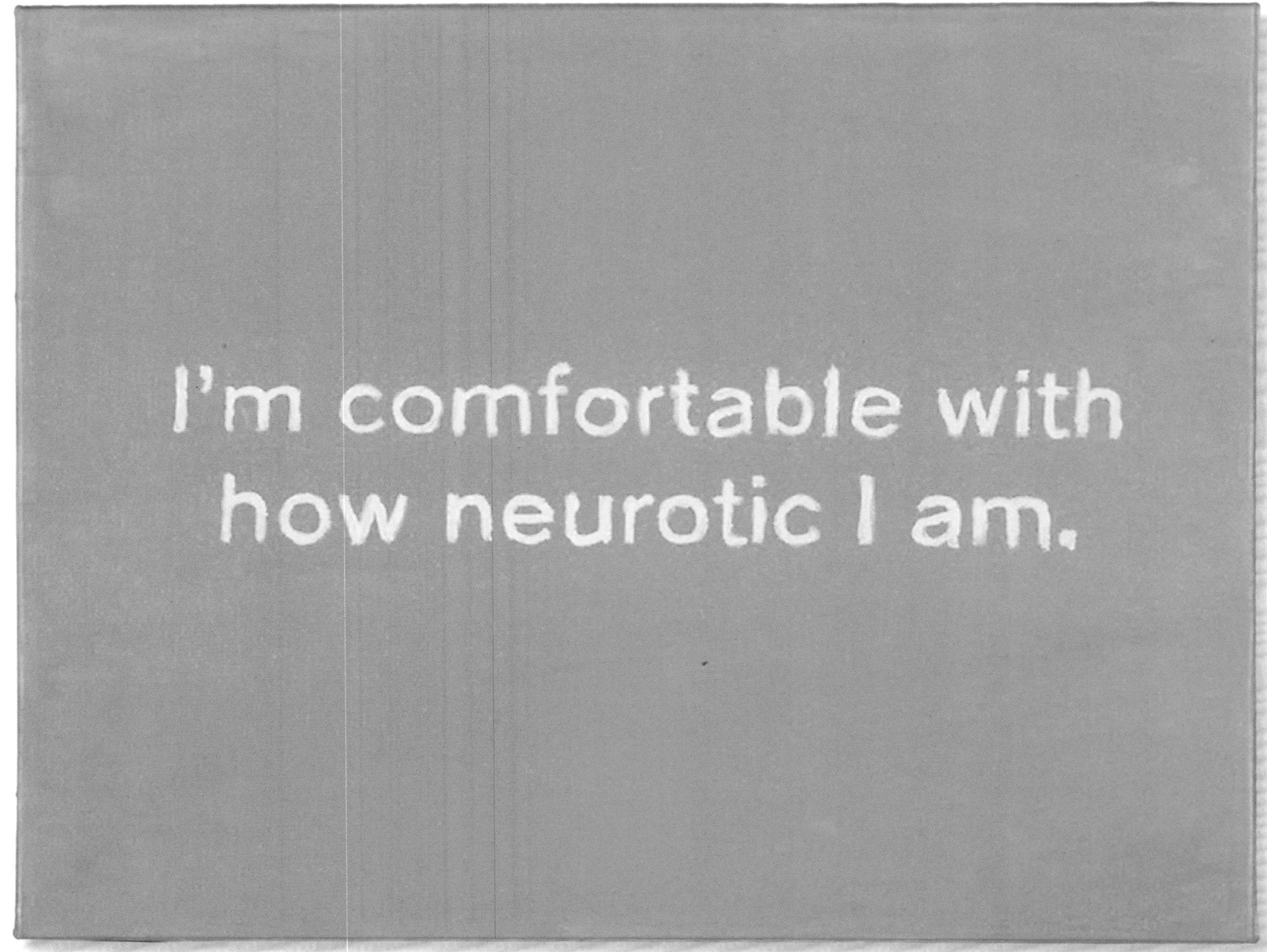

The Thoughts in My Head #51
2014
Acrylic on Canvas
11 x 14 inches

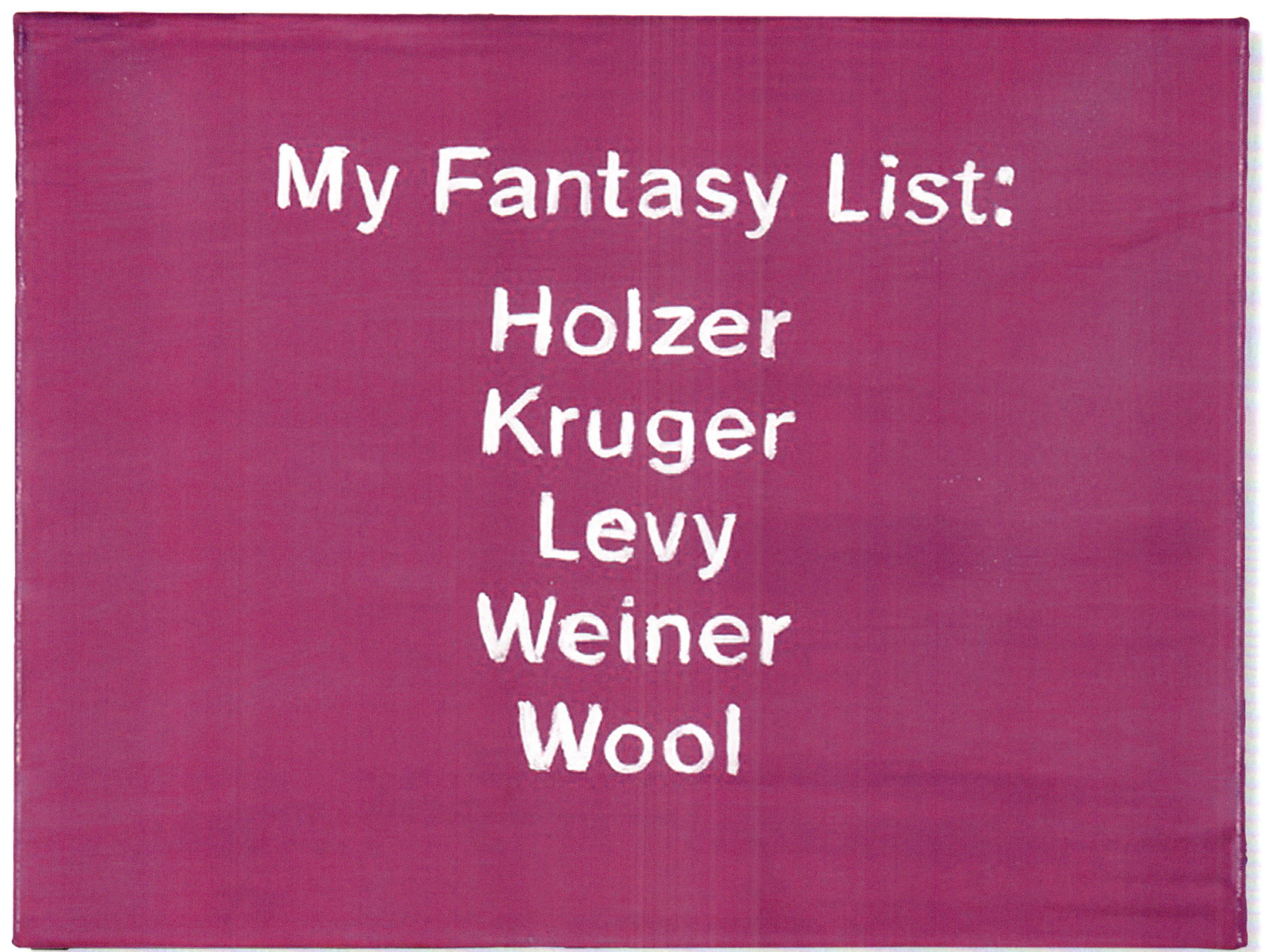

The Thoughts in My Head #52
2014
Acrylic on Canvas
11 x 14 inches

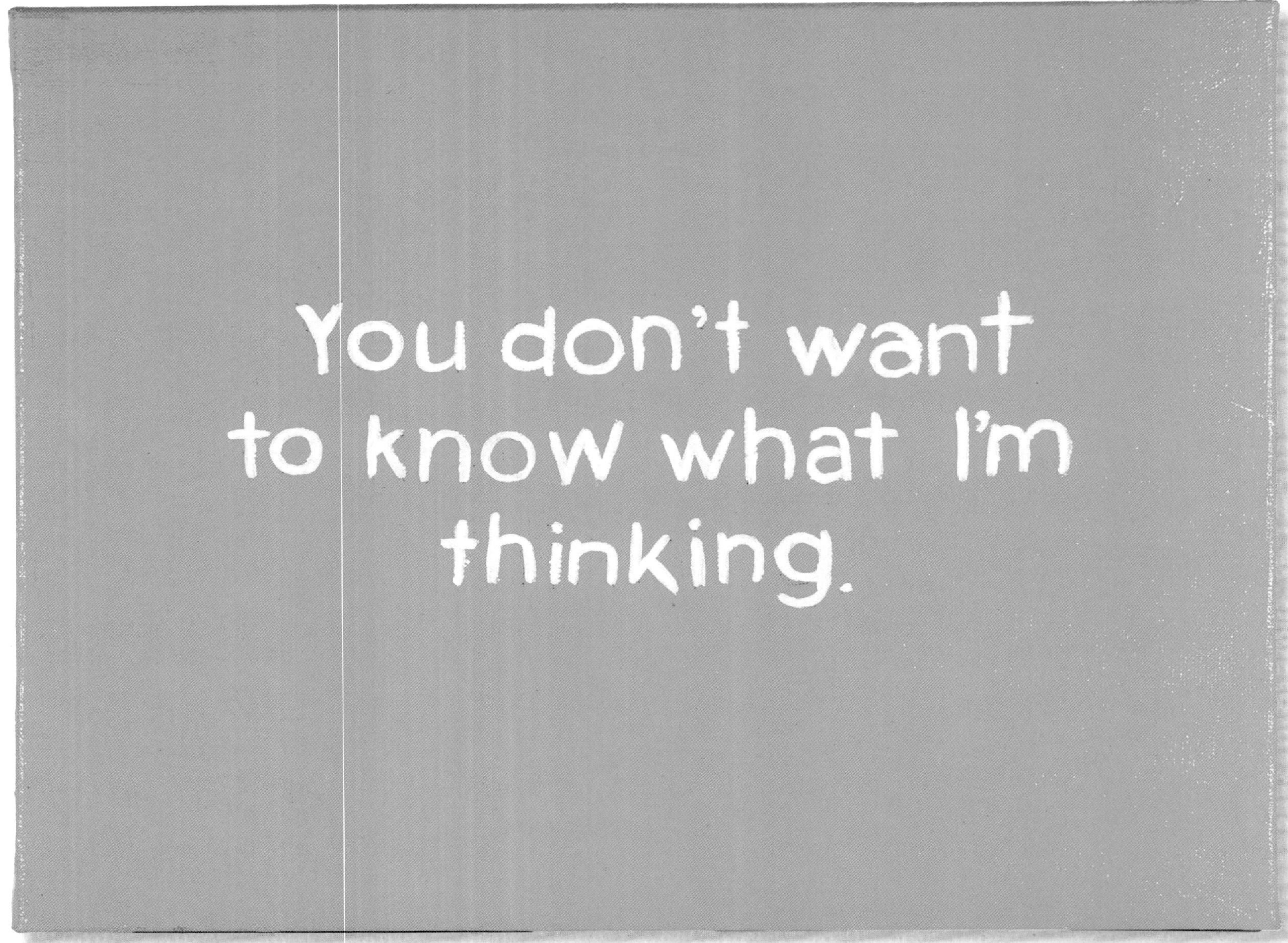

The Thoughts in My Head #53
2014
Acrylic on Canvas
11 x 14 inches

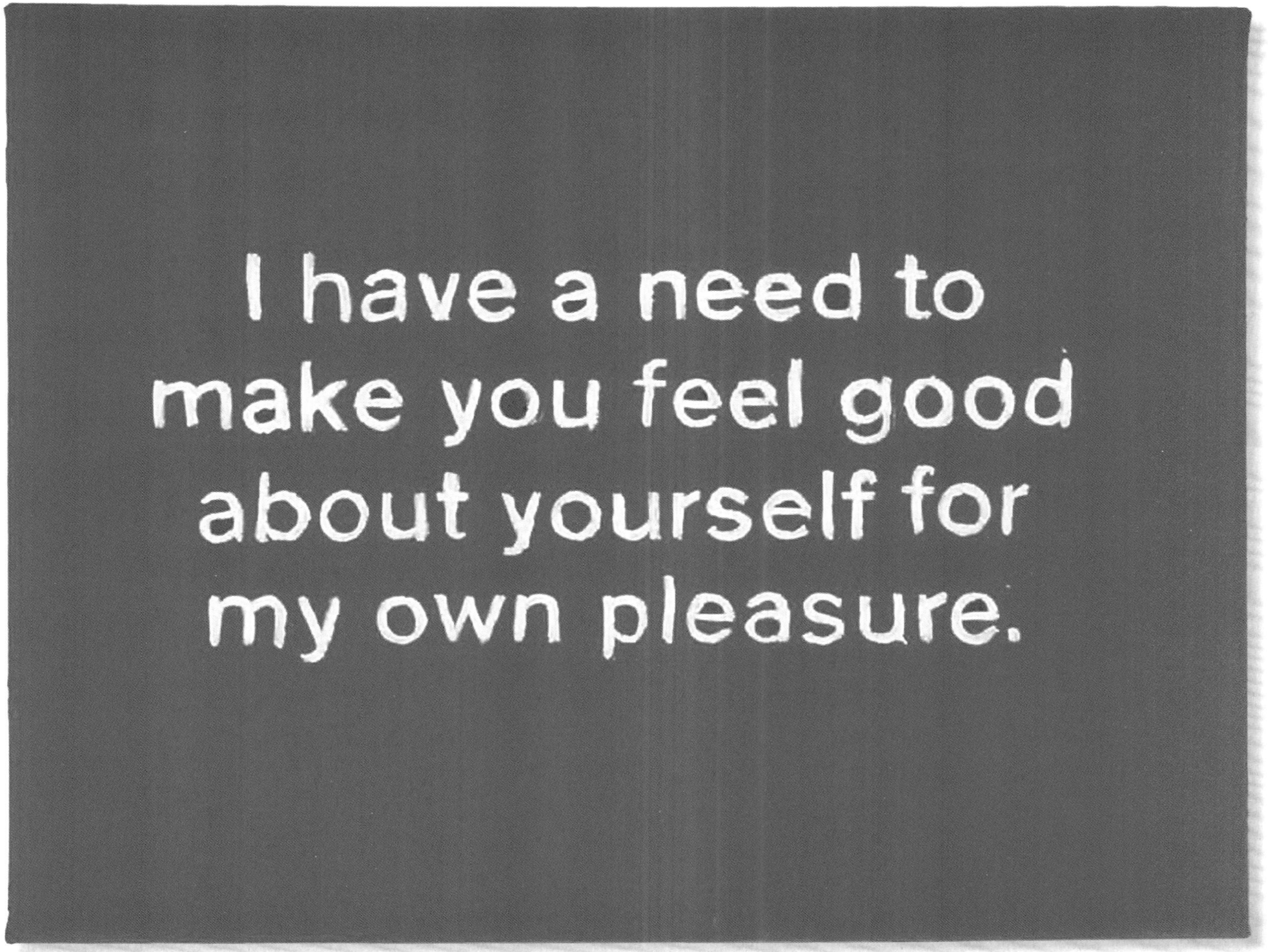

I have a need to
make you feel good
about yourself for
my own pleasure.

The Thoughts in My Head #54
2014
Acrylic on Canvas
11 x 14 inches

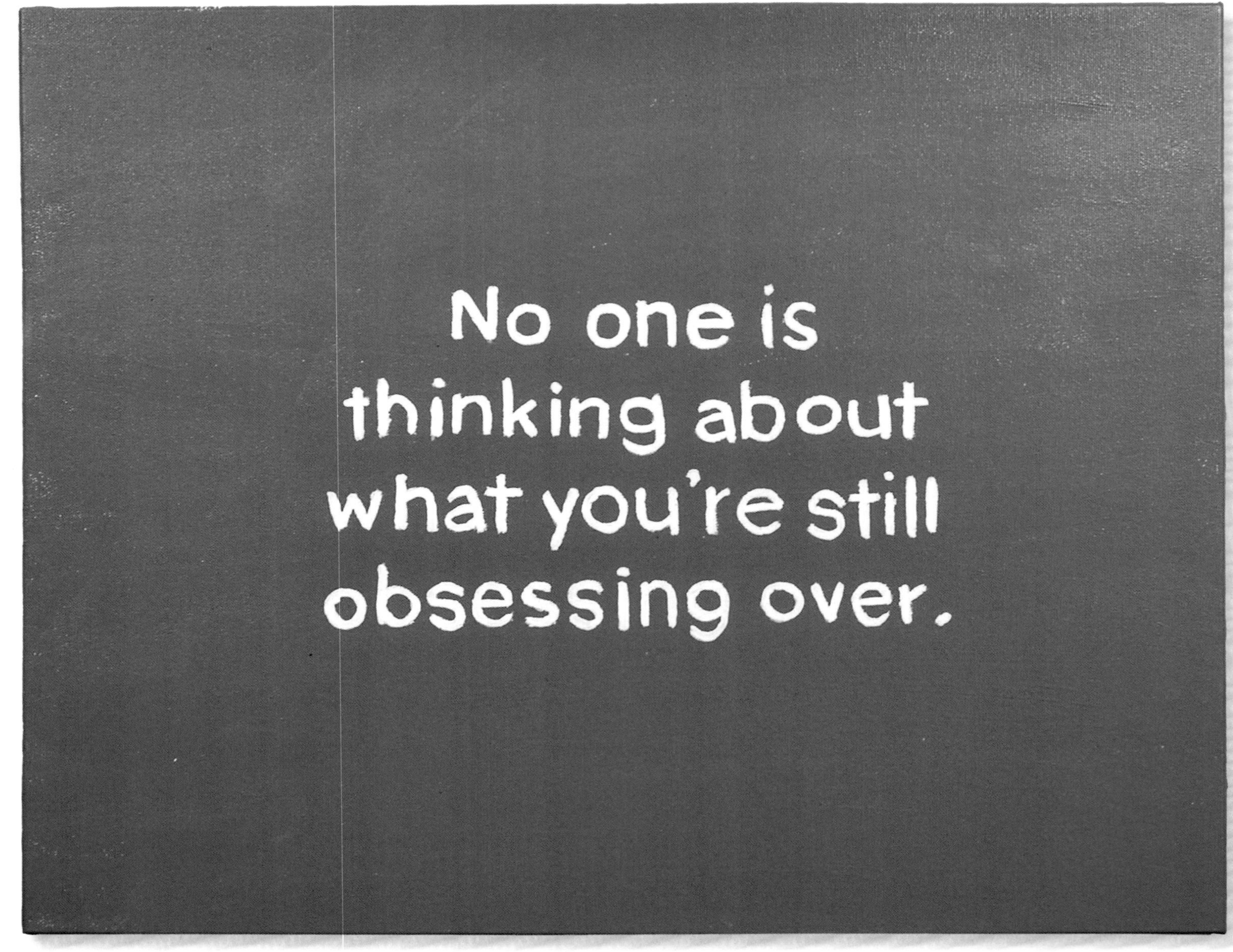

The Thoughts in My Head #55
2014
Acrylic on Canvas
11 x 14 inches

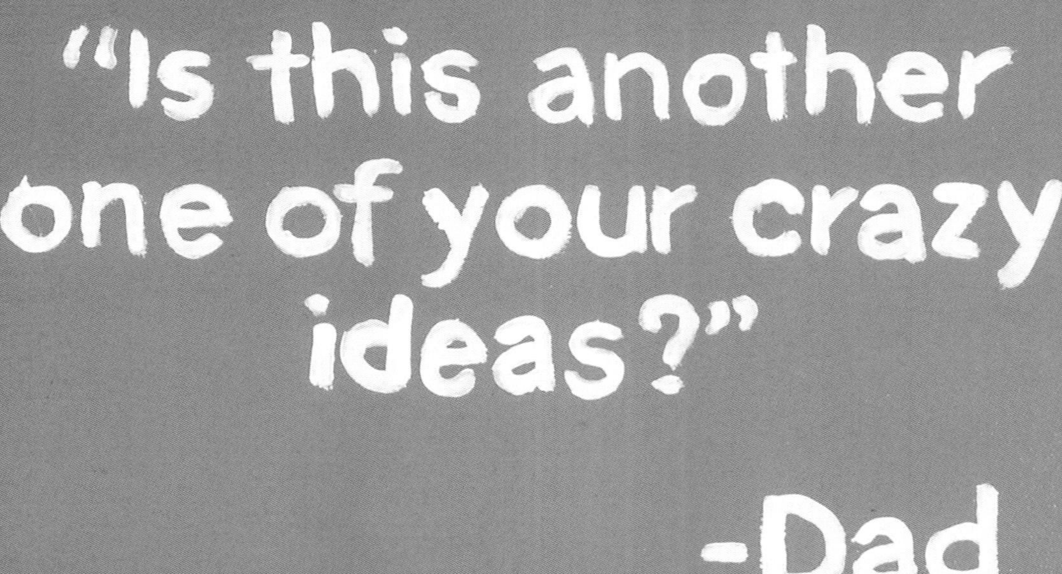

The Thoughts in My Head #56
2015
Acrylic on Canvas
11 x 14 inches

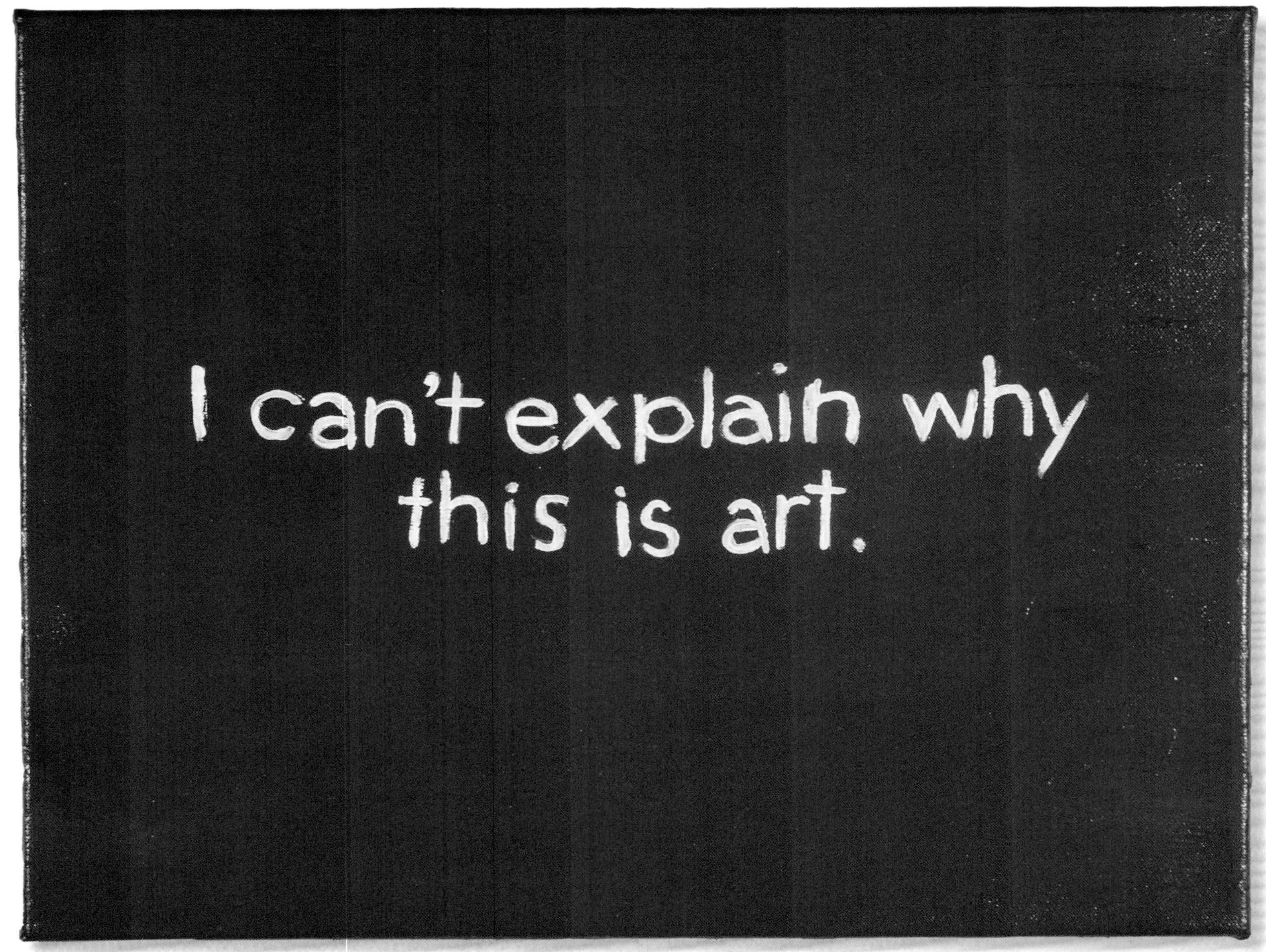

The Thoughts in My Head #57
2015
Acrylic on Canvas
11 x 14 inches

The Thoughts in My Head #58
2016
Acrylic on Canvas
11 x 14 inches

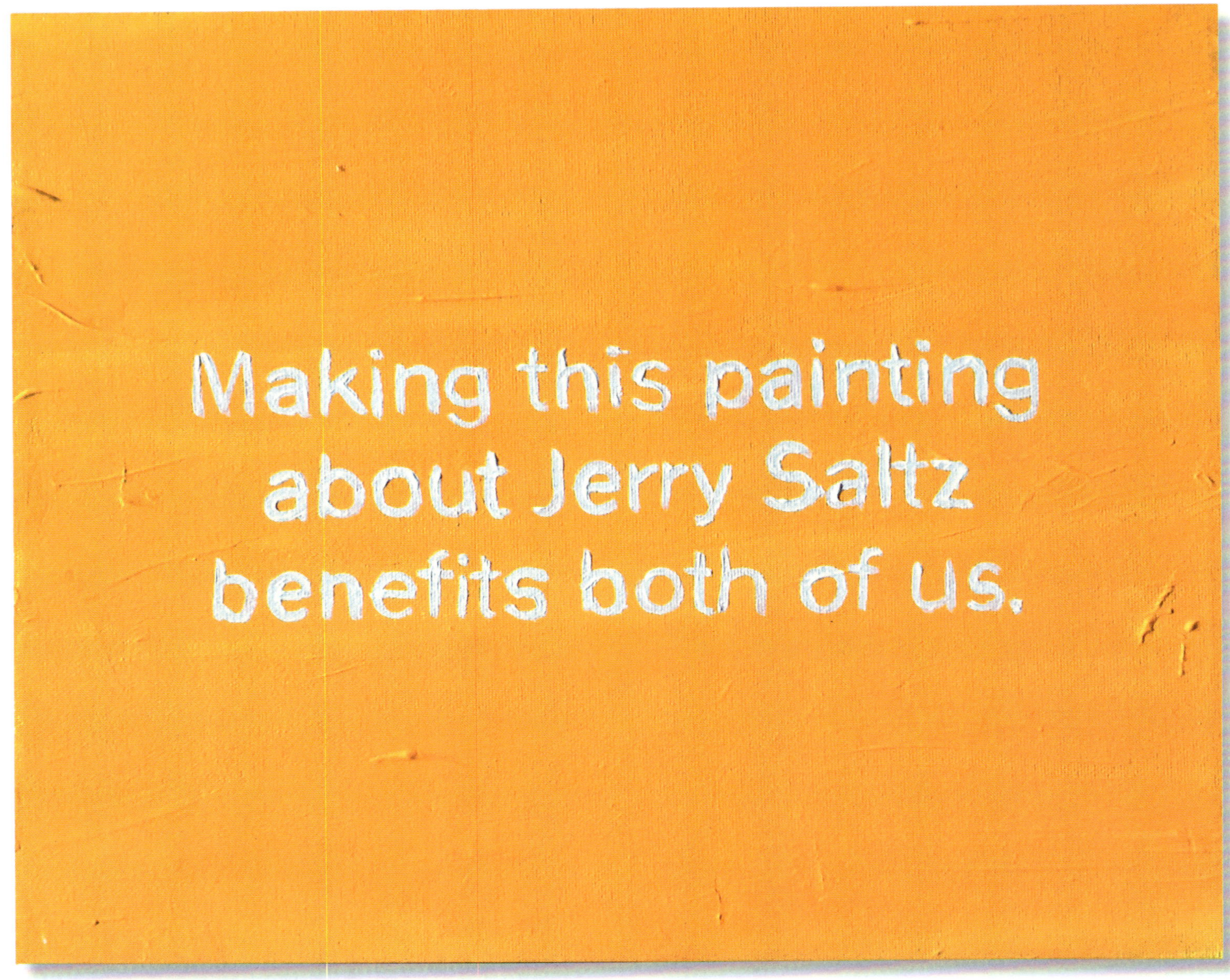

The Thoughts in My Head #59
2016
Acrylic on Canvas
11 x 14 inches

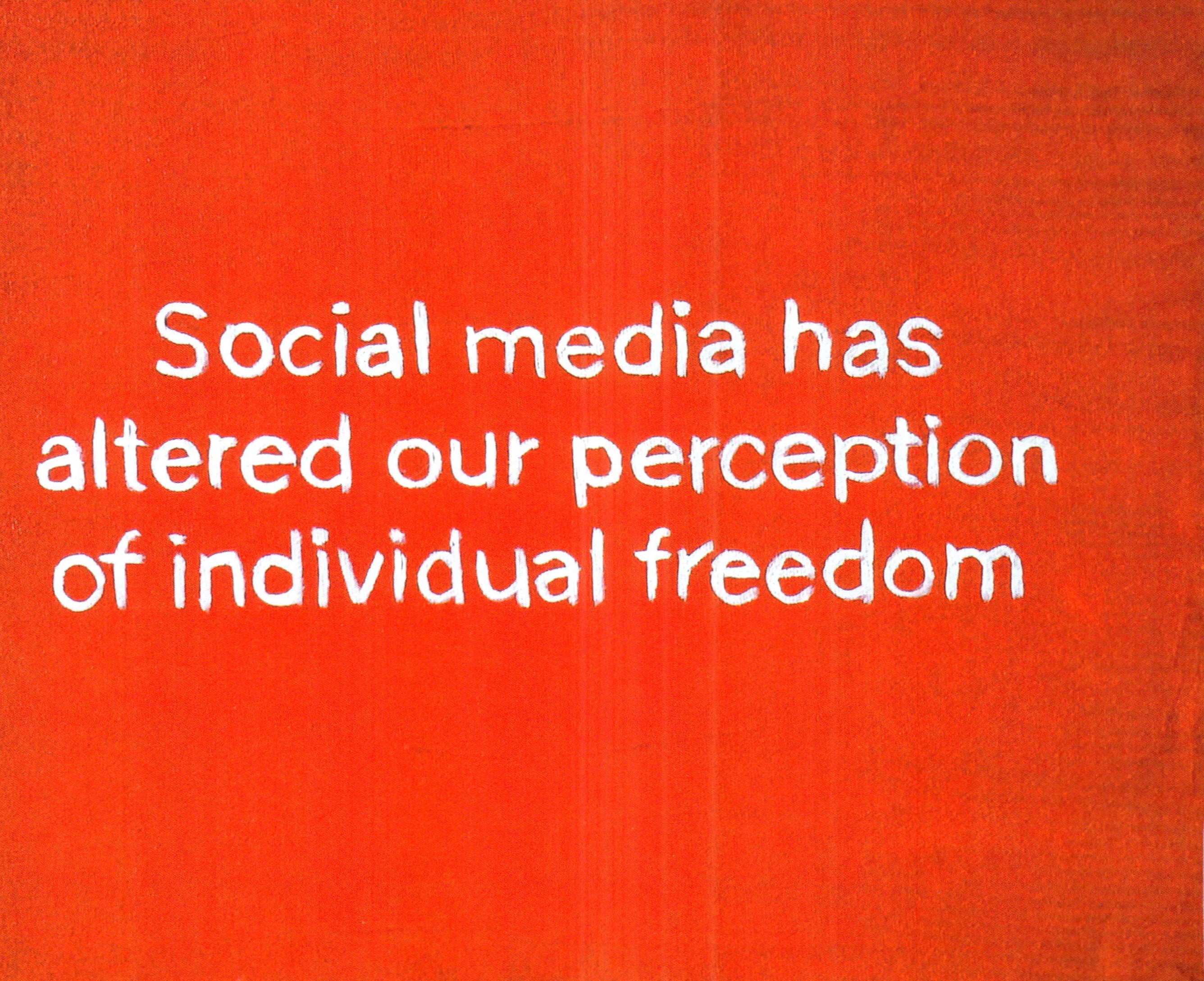

The Thoughts in My Head #60
2016
Acrylic on Canvas
11 x 14 inches

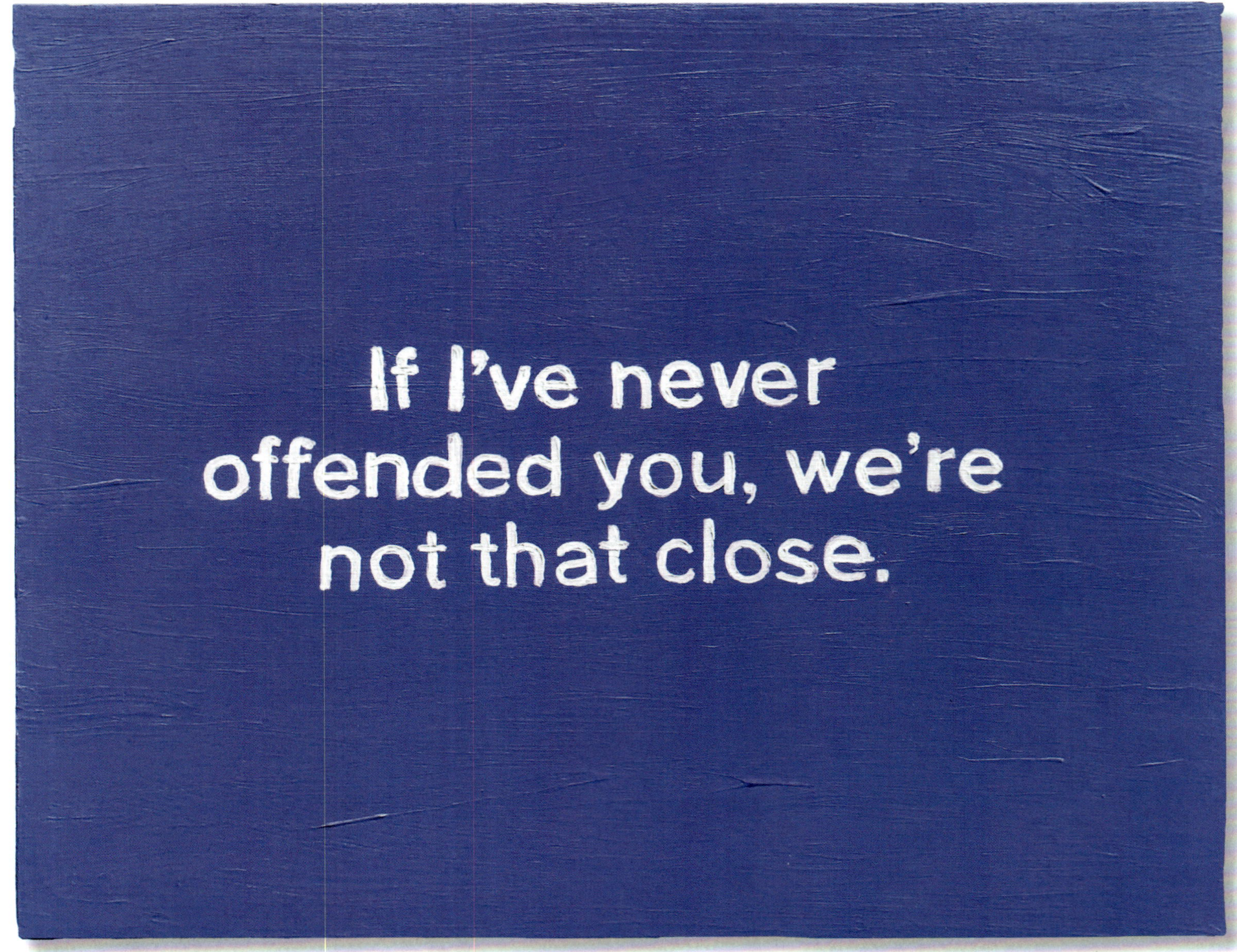

The Thoughts in My Head #61
2016
Acrylic on Canvas
11 x 14 inches

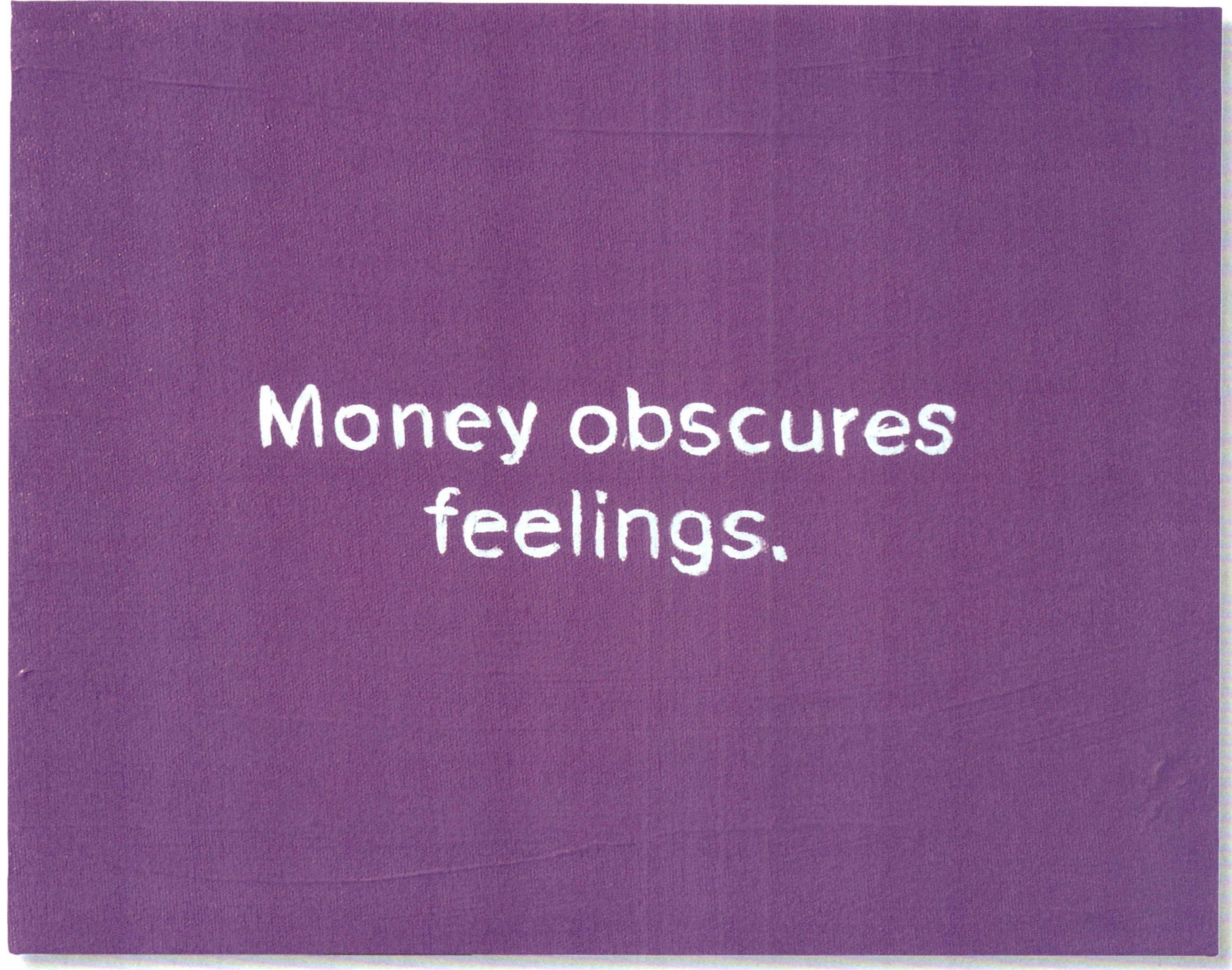

The Thoughts in My Head #62
2016
Acrylic on Canvas
11 x 14 inches

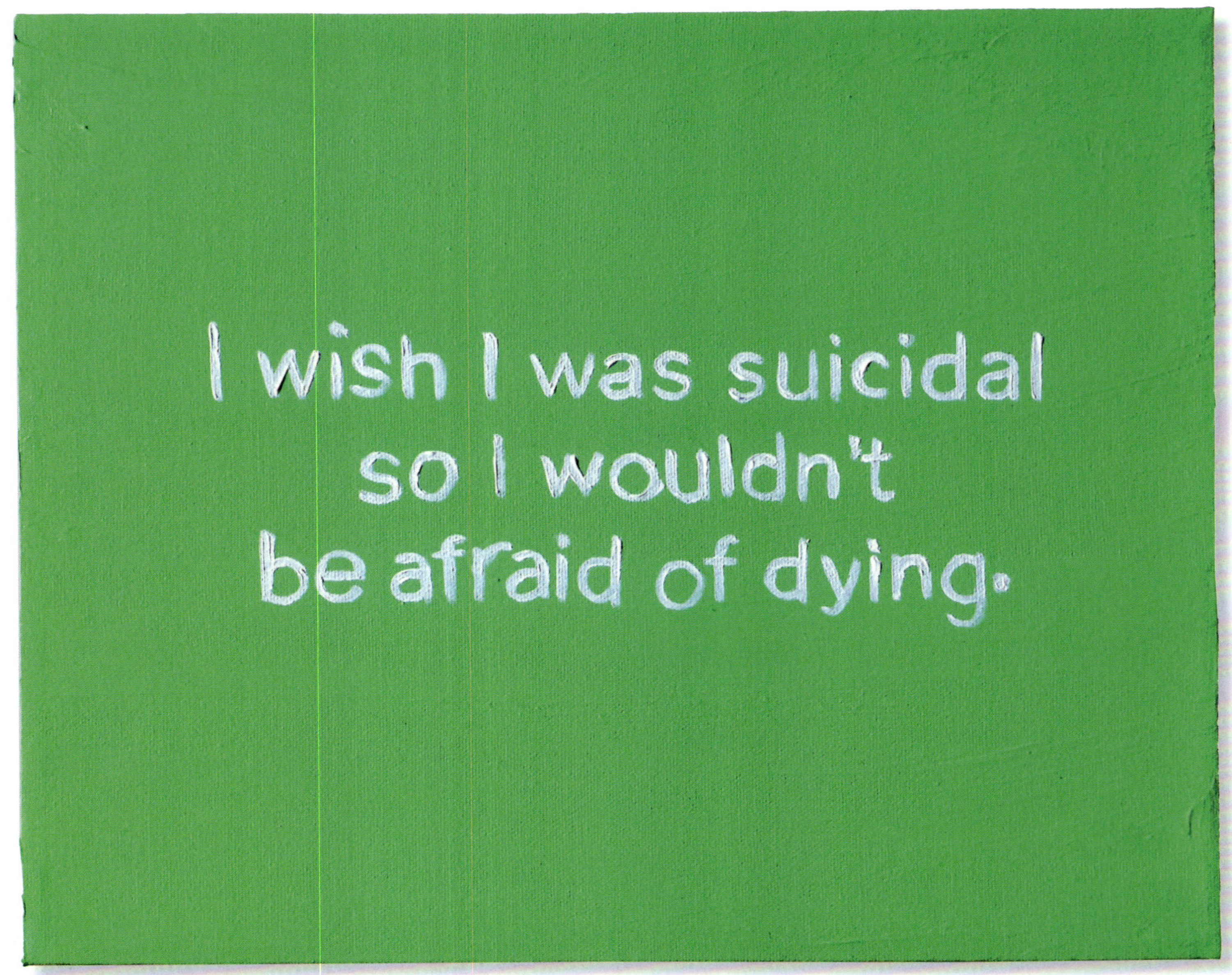

The Thoughts in My Head #63
2016
Acrylic on Canvas
11 x 14 inches

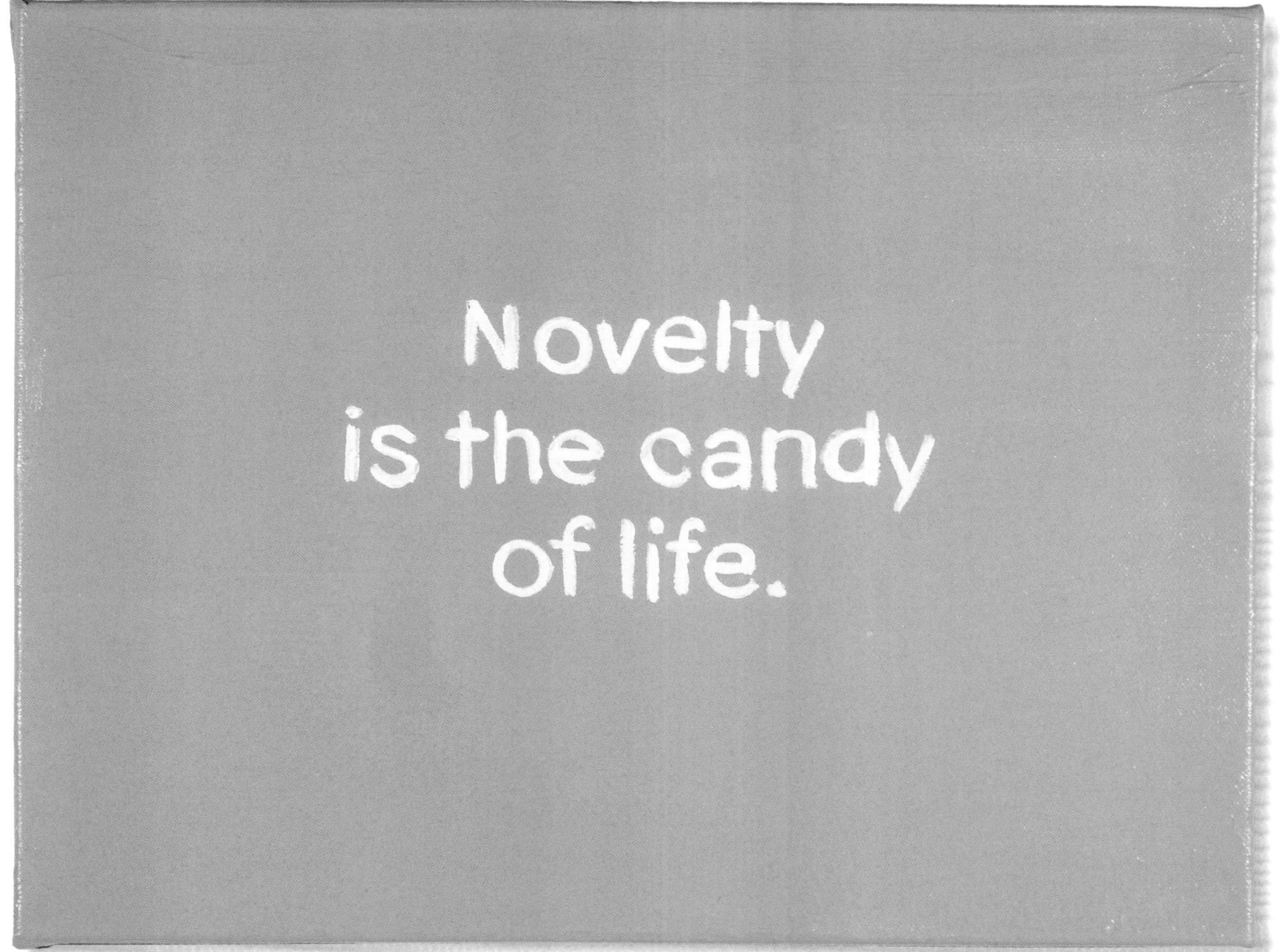

The Thoughts in My Head #64
2016
Acrylic on Canvas
11 x 14 inches

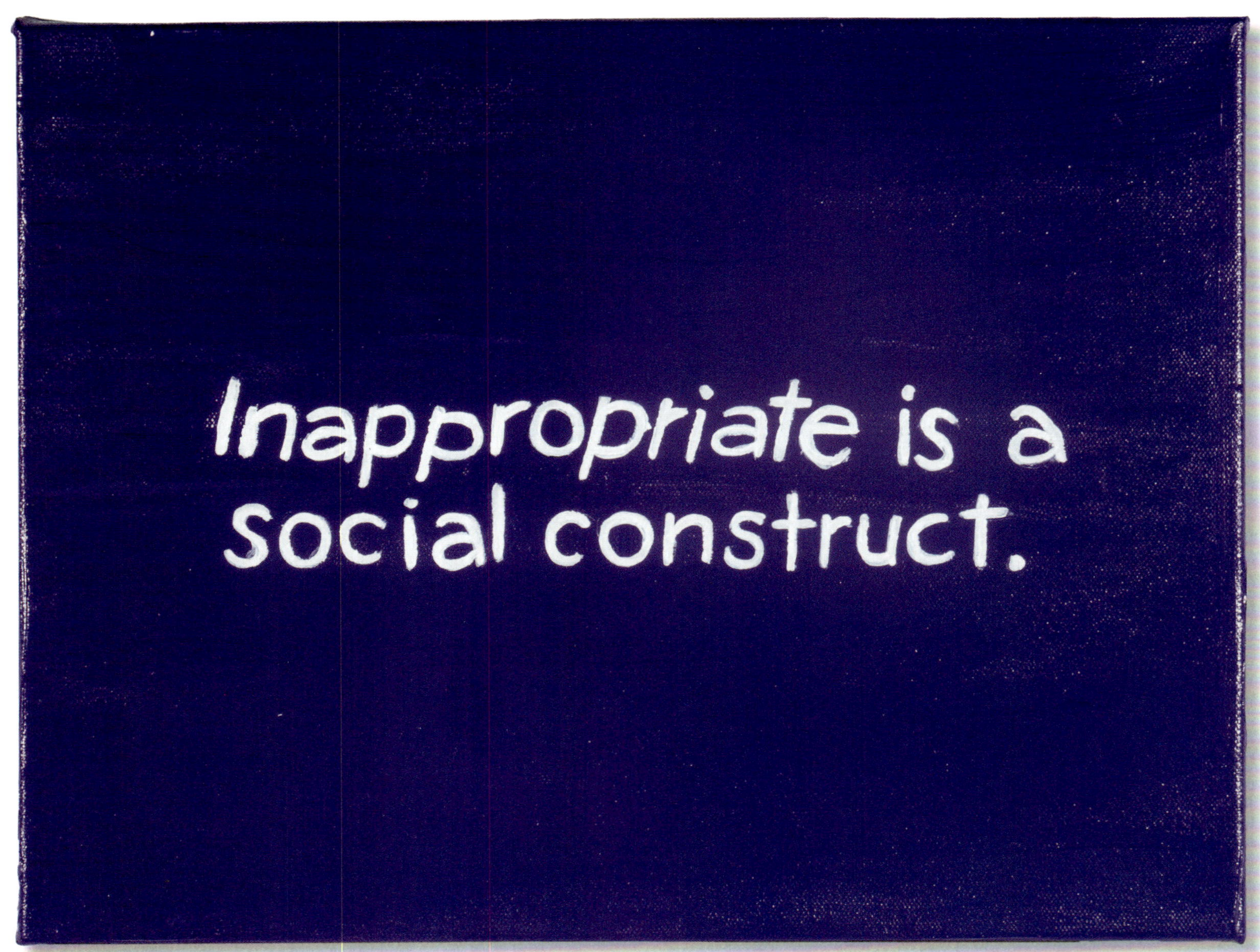

The Thoughts in My Head #65
2016
Acrylic on Canvas
11 x 14 inches

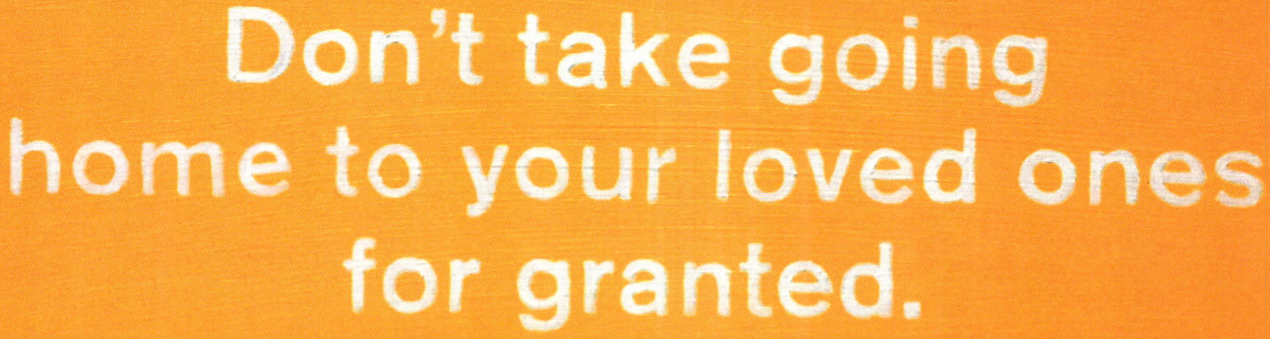

The Thoughts in My Head #66
2016
Acrylic on Canvas
11 x 14 inches

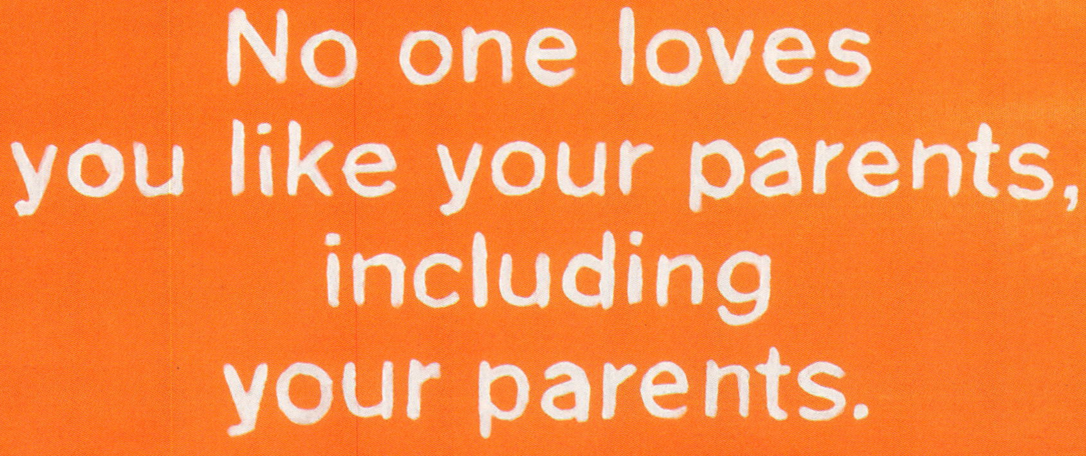

The Thoughts in My Head #67
2017
Acrylic on Canvas
11 x 14 inches

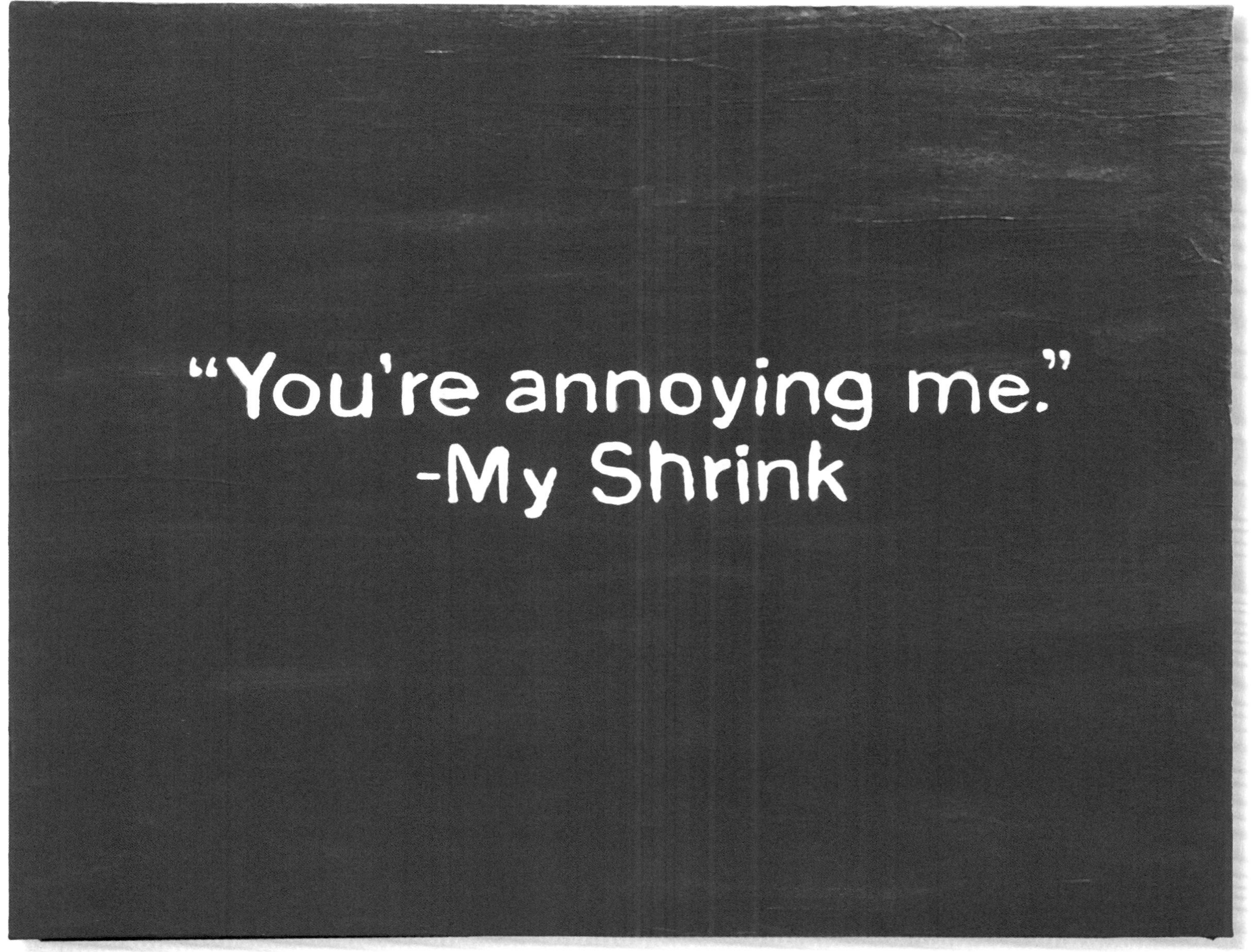

The Thoughts in My Head #68
2017
Acrylic on Canvas
11 x 14 inches

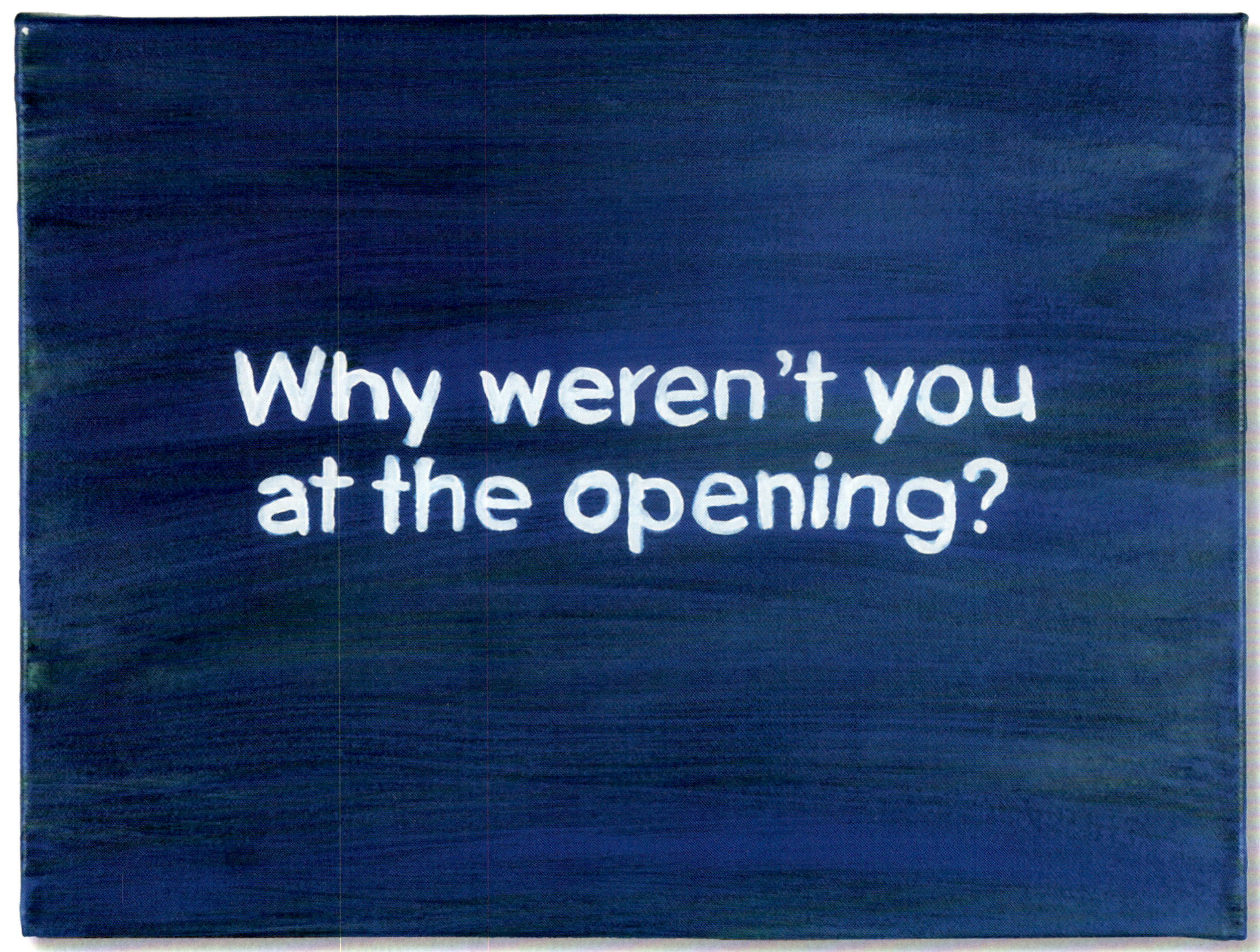

The Thoughts in My Head #69
2017
Acrylic on Canvas
11 x 14 inches

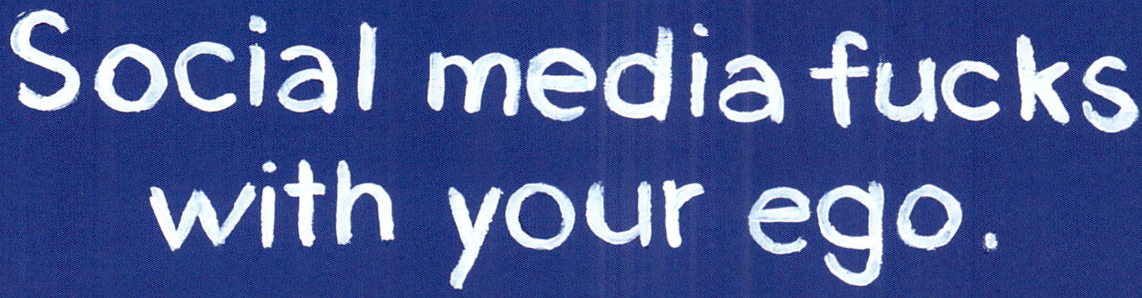

The Thoughts in My Head #70
2018
Acrylic on Canvas
11 x 14 inches

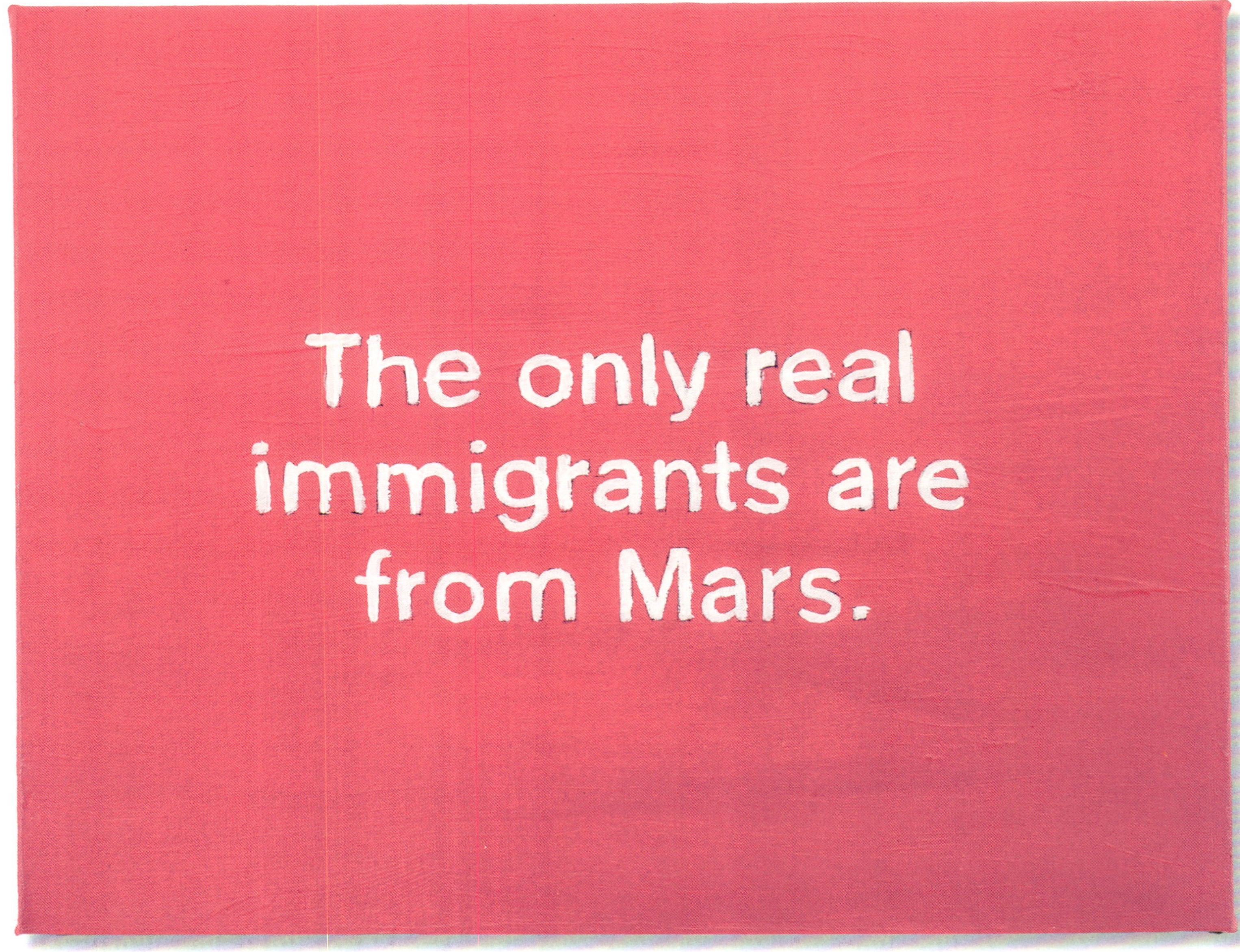

The Thoughts in My Head #71
2018
Acrylic on Canvas
11 x 14 inches

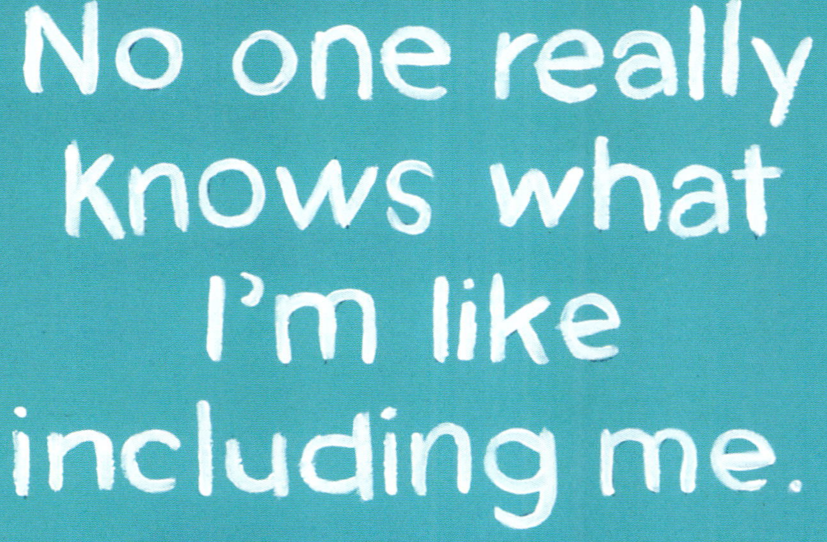

The Thoughts in My Head #72
2018
Acrylic on Canvas
11 x 14 inches

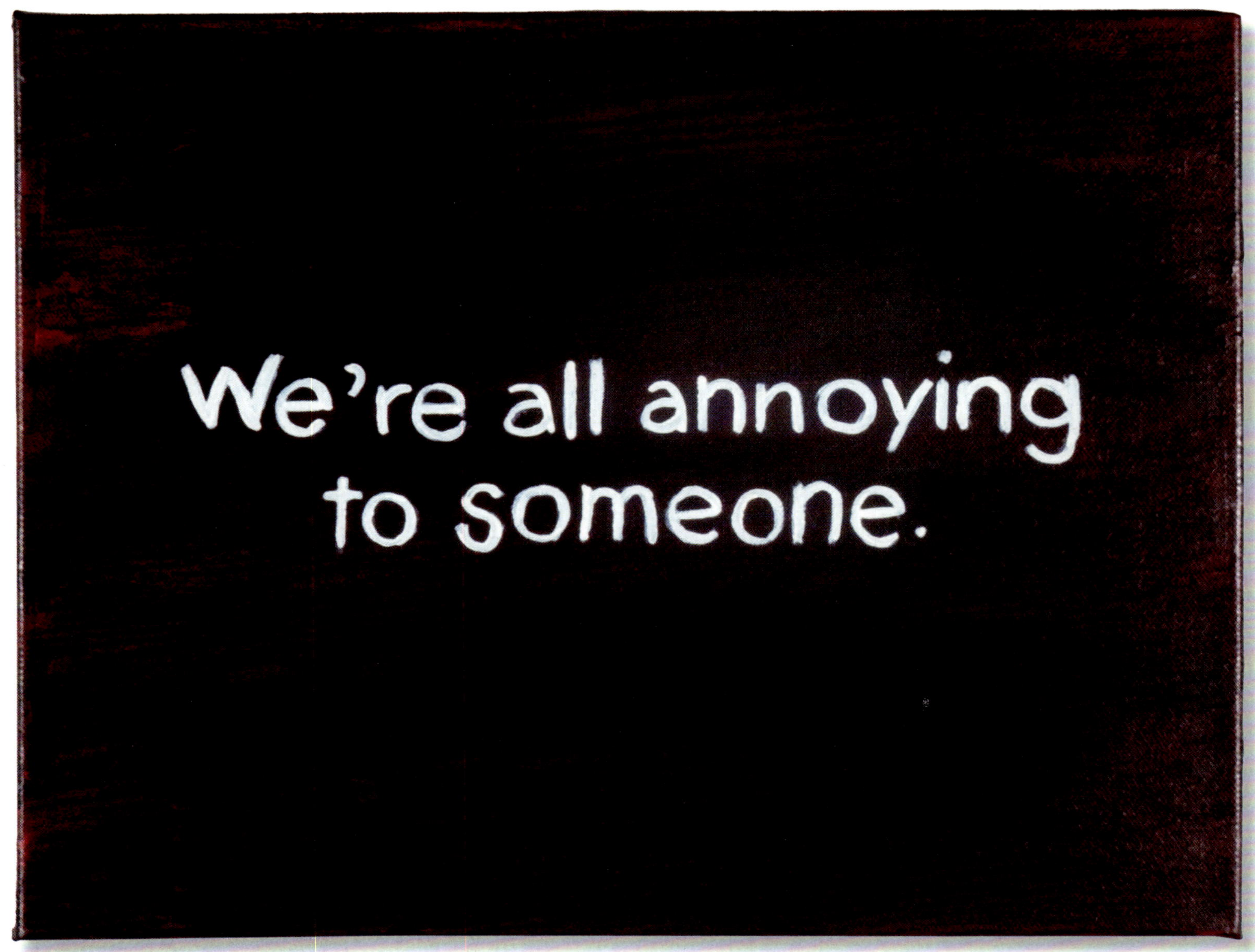

The Thoughts in My Head #73
2018
Acrylic on Canvas
11 x 14 inches

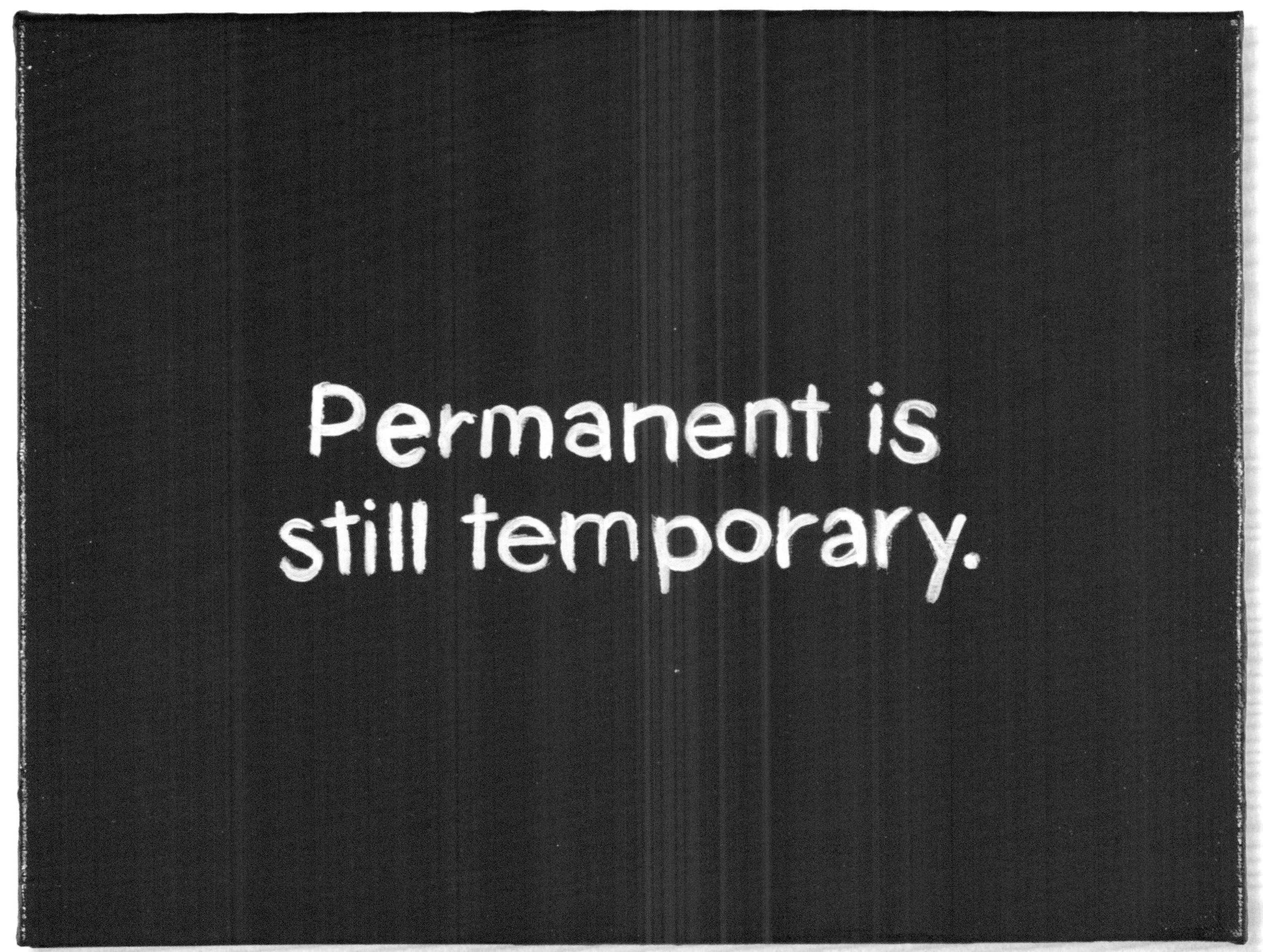

The Thoughts in My Head #74
2018
Acrylic on Canvas
11 x 14 inches

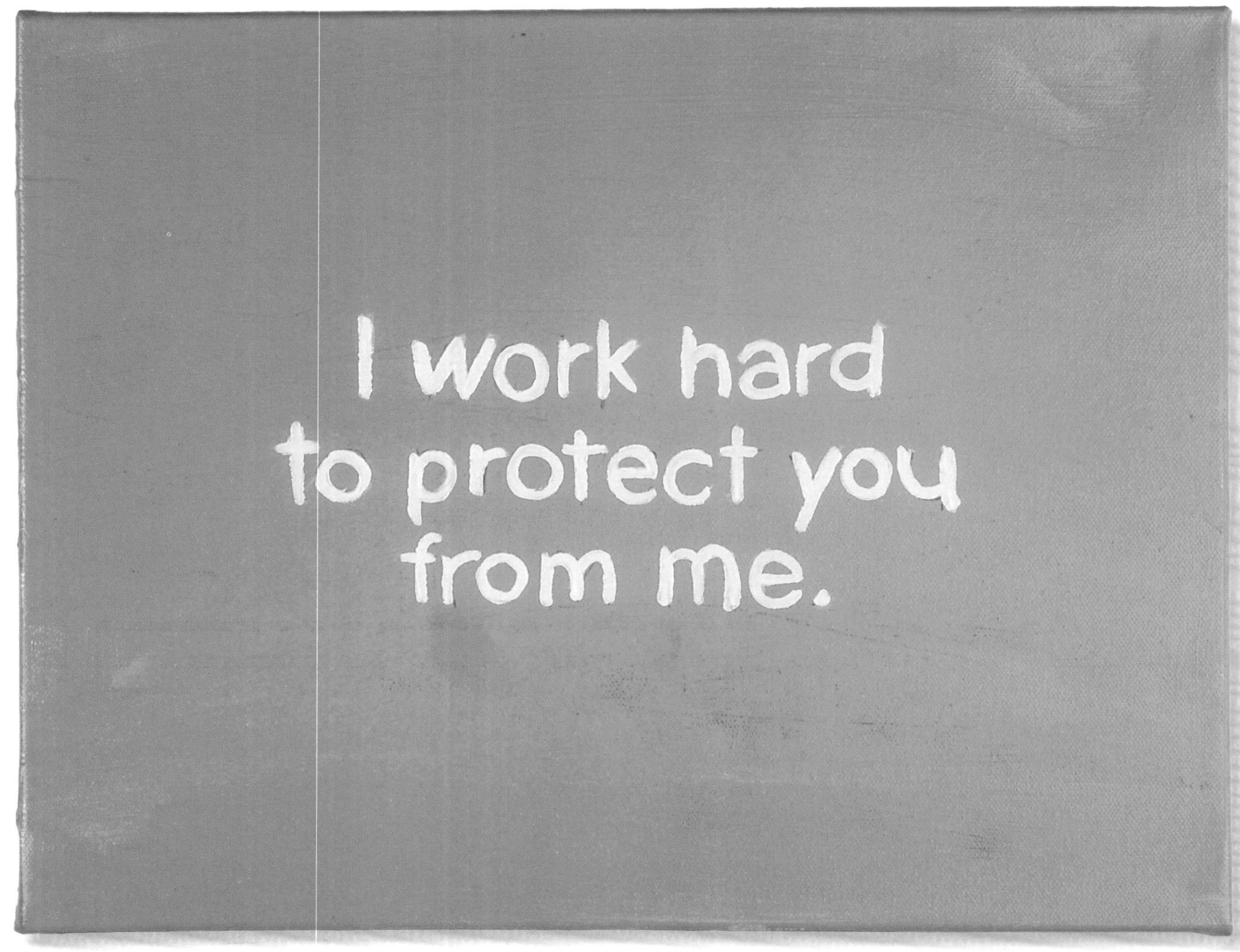

The Thoughts in My Head #75
2018
Acrylic on Canvas
11 x 14 inches

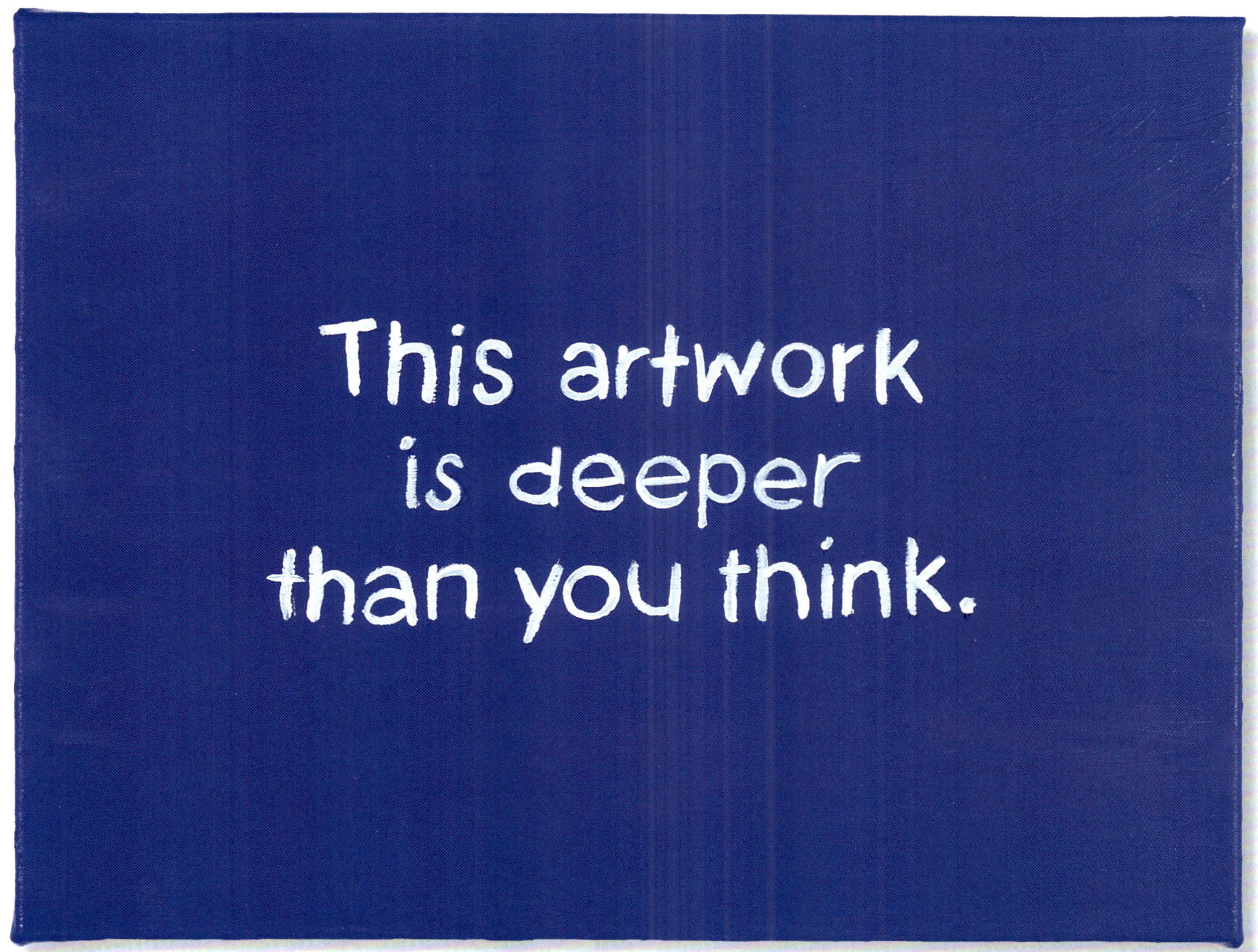

The Thoughts in My Head #76
2019
Acrylic on Canvas
11 x 14 inches

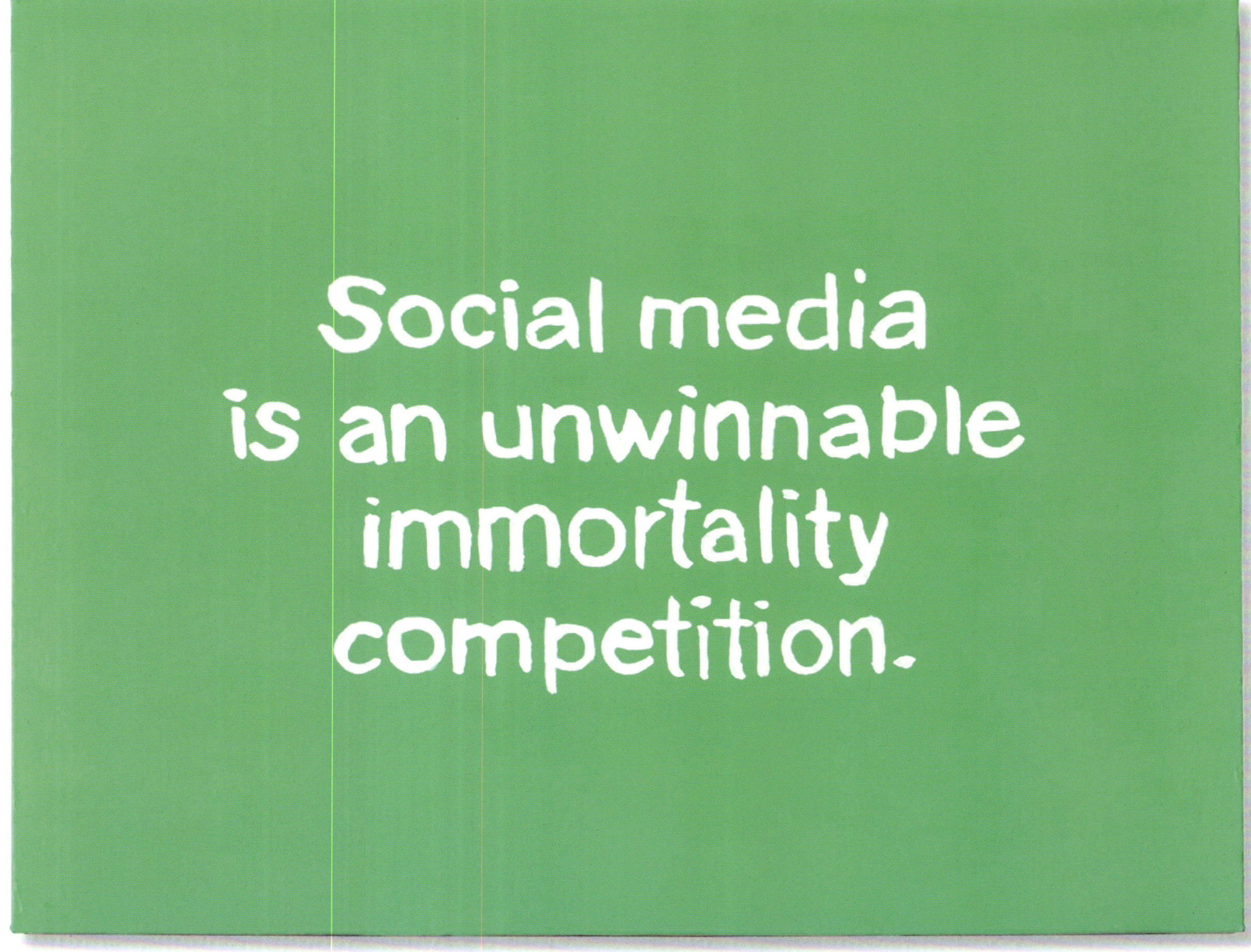

The Thoughts in My Head #77
2019
Acrylic on Canvas
11 x 14 inches

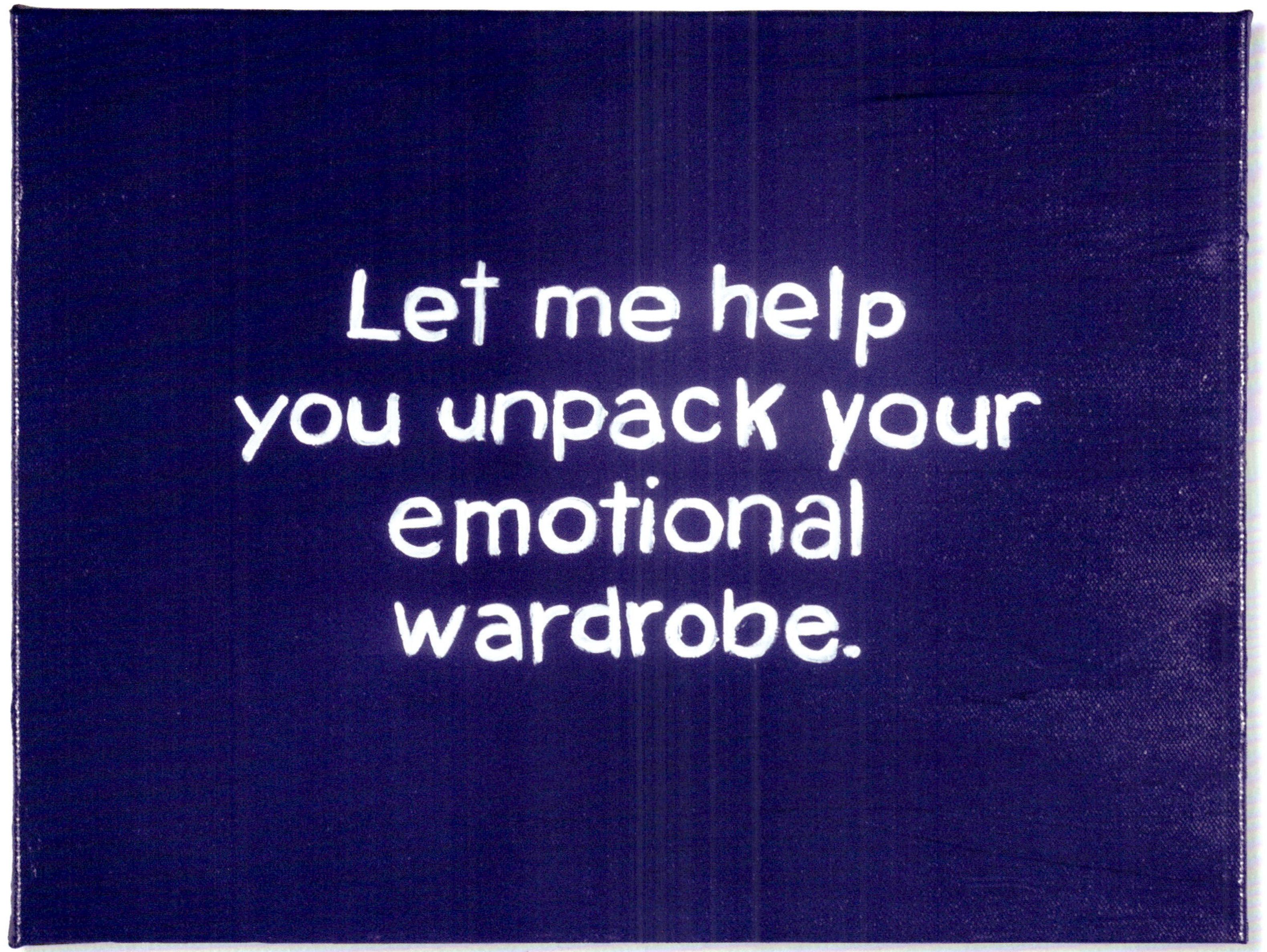

The Thoughts in My Head #78
2019
Acrylic on Canvas
11 x 14 inches

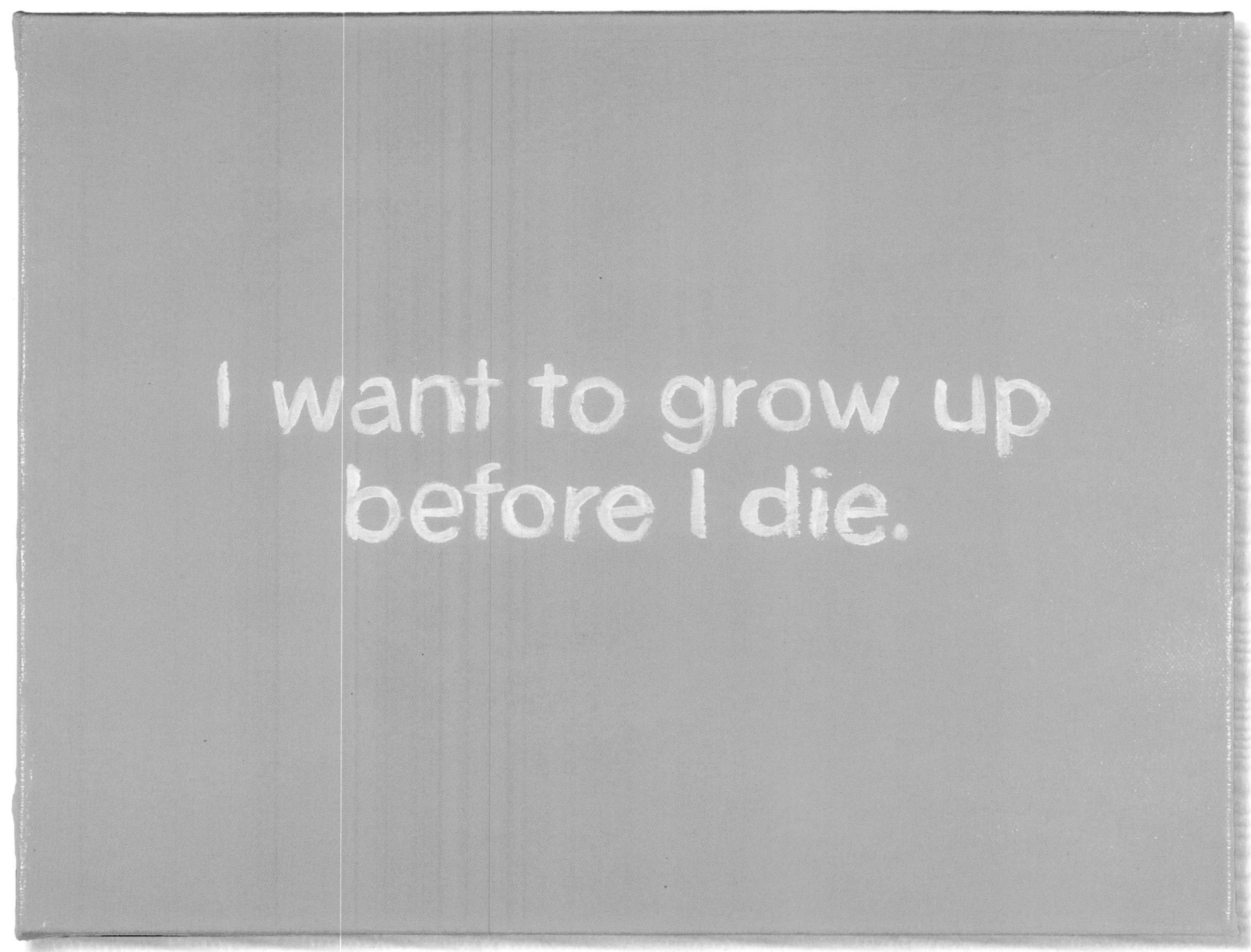

The Thoughts in My Head #79
2019
Acrylic on Canvas
11 x 14 inches

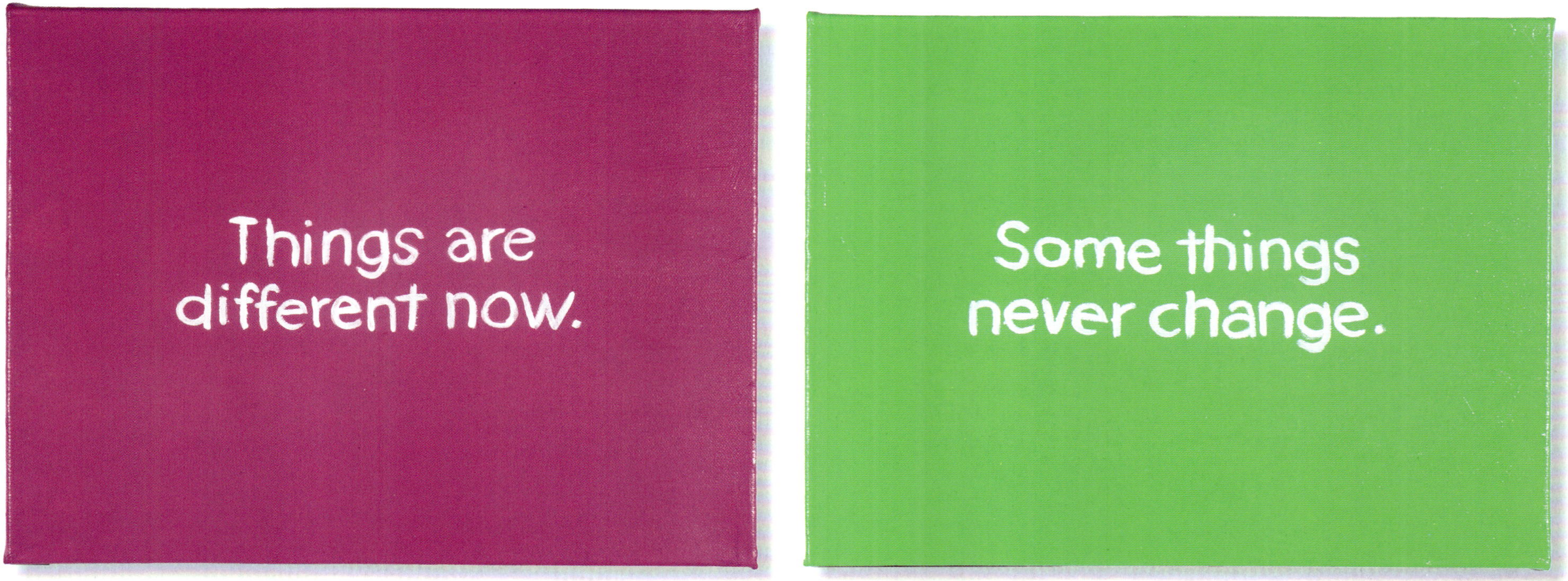

Things are
different now.

Some things
never change.

The Thoughts in My Head #80 (a+b)
2012
Acrylic on Canvas
11 x 14 inches

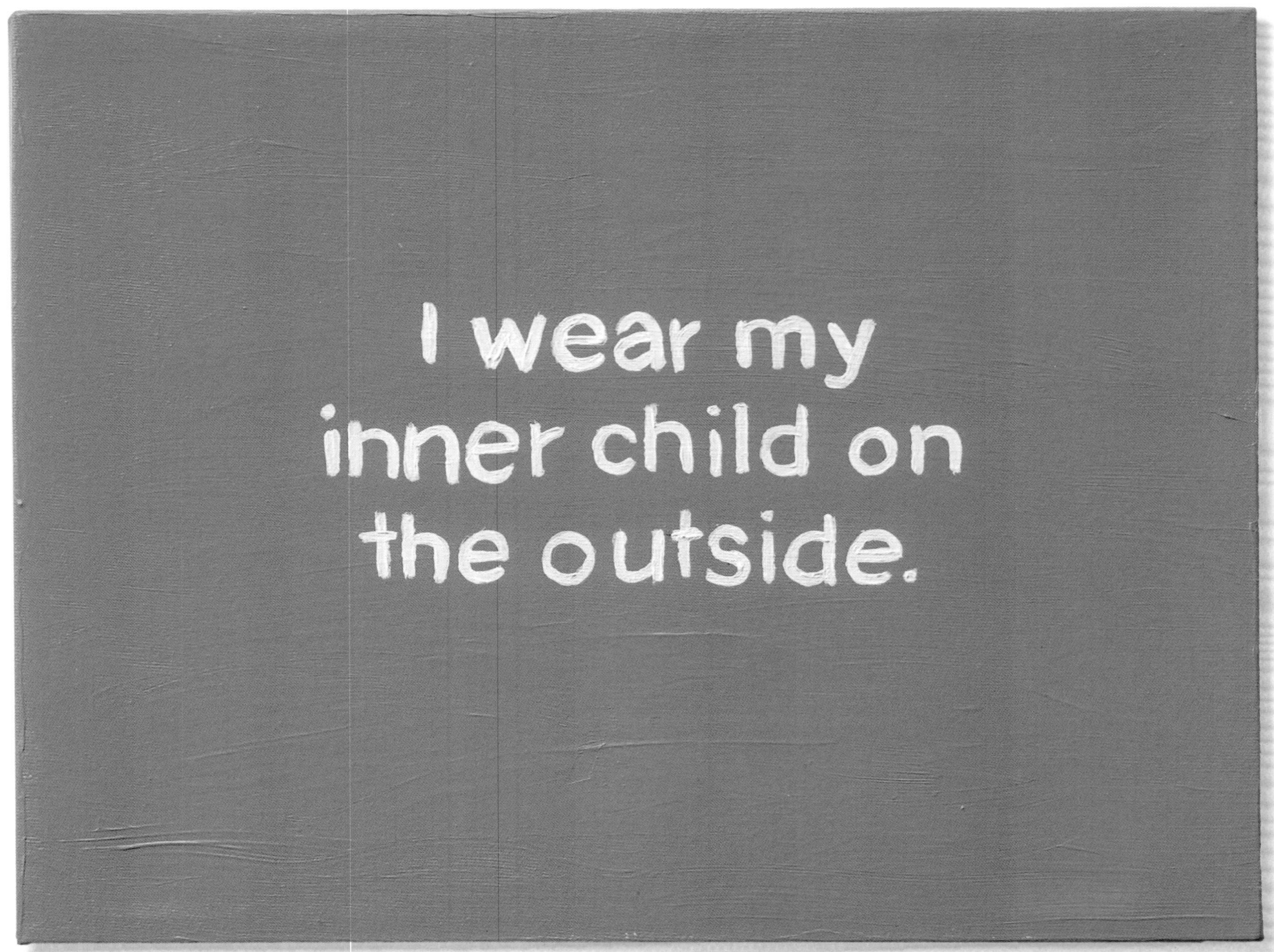

The Thoughts in My Head #81
2019
Acrylic on Canvas
11 x 14 inches

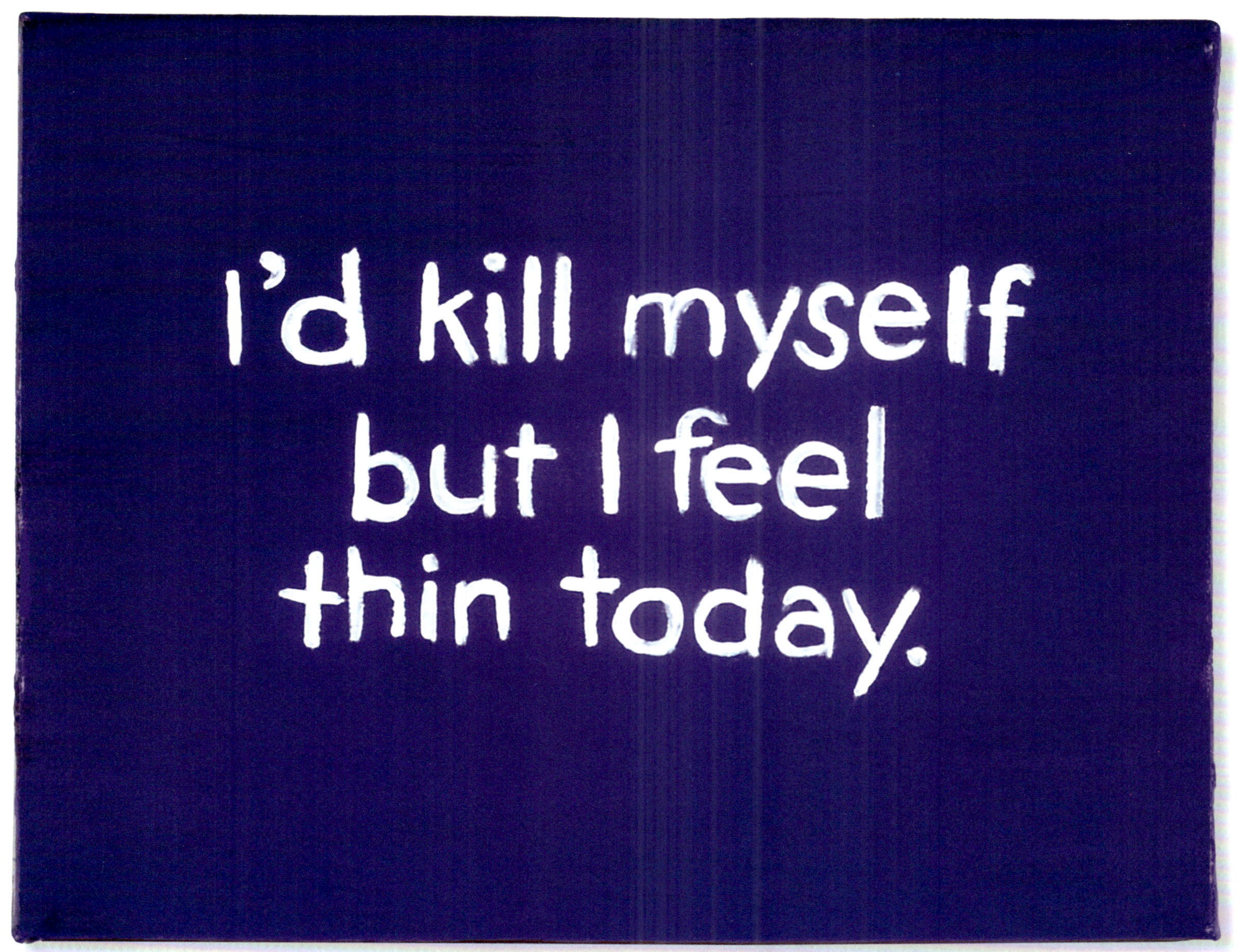

The Thoughts in My Head #82
2019
Acrylic on Canvas
11 x 14 inches

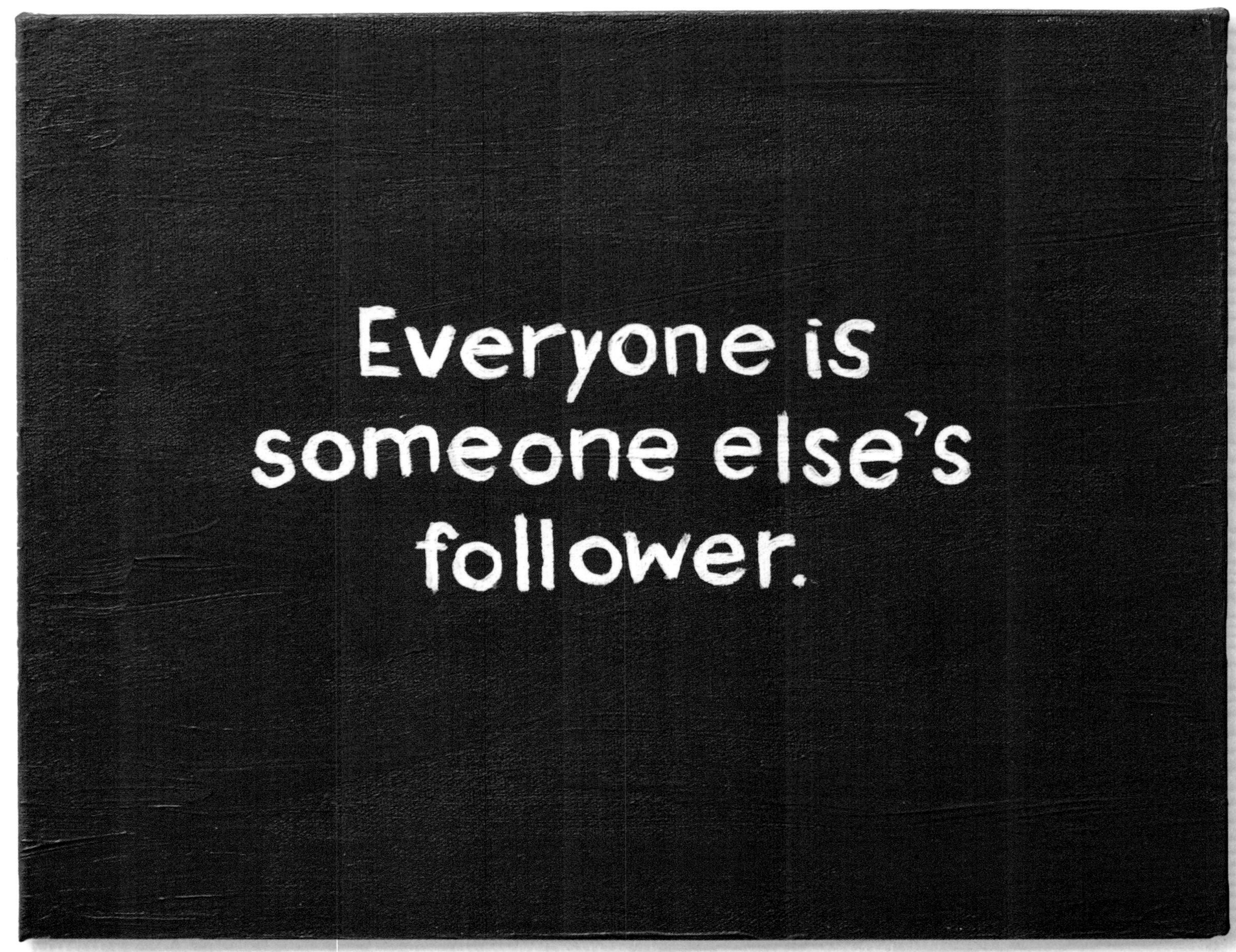

The Thoughts in My Head #83
2019
Acrylic on Canvas
11 x 14 inches

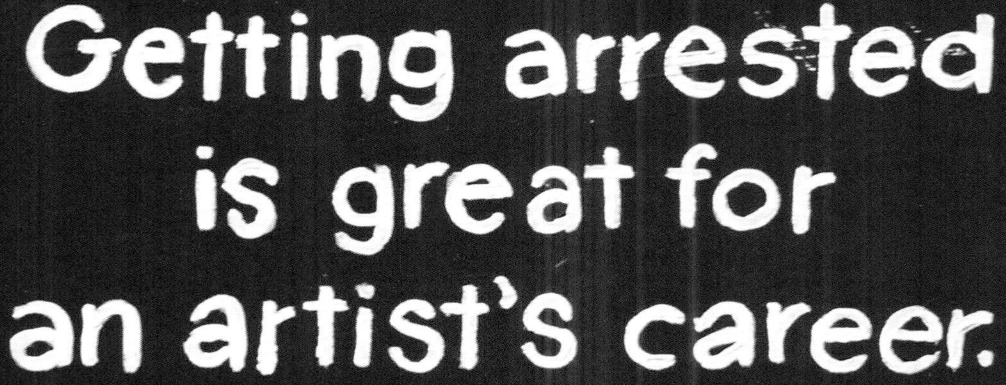

The Thoughts in My Head #84
2019
Acrylic on Canvas
11 x 14 inches

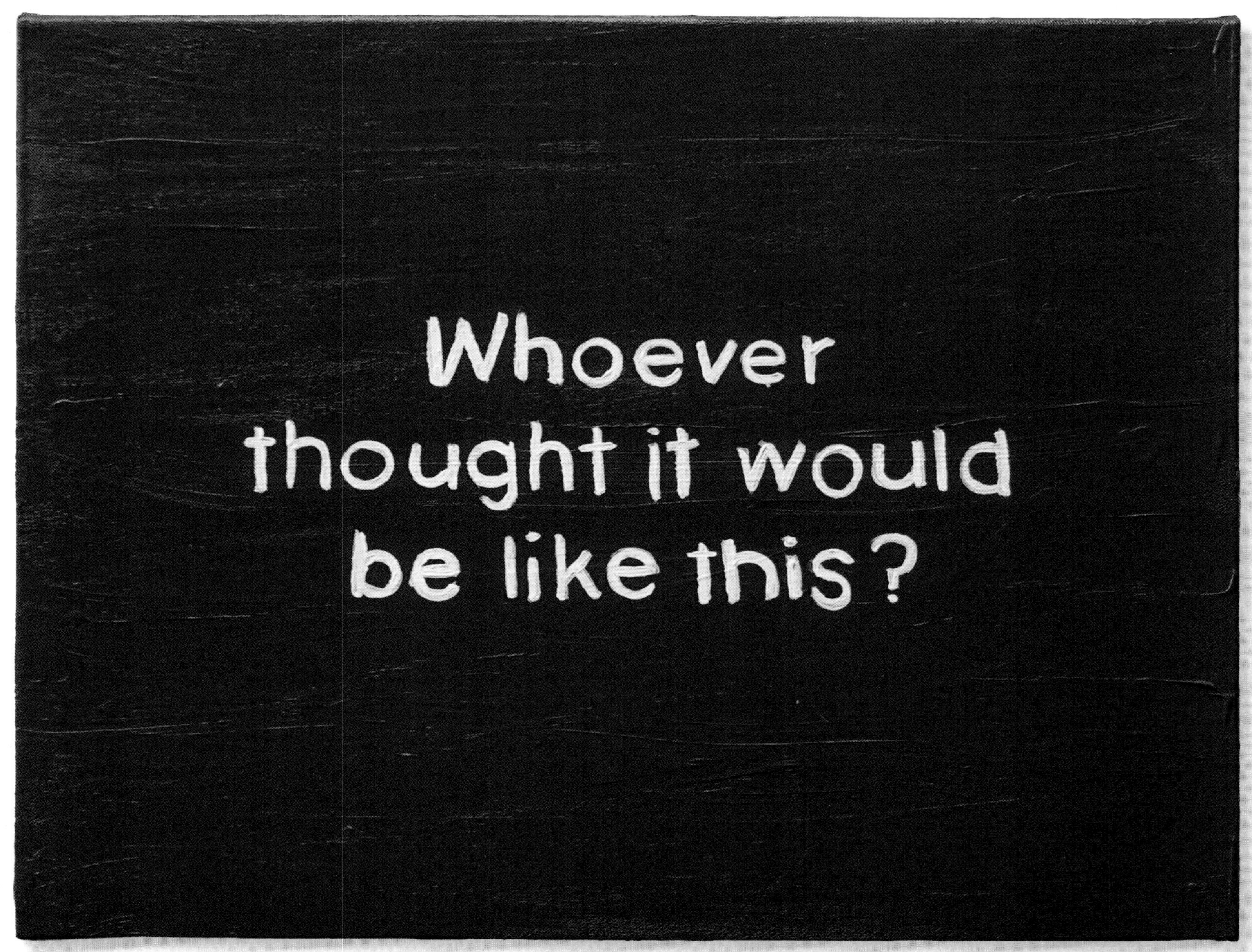

The Thoughts in My Head #85
2019
Acrylic on Canvas
11 x 14 inches

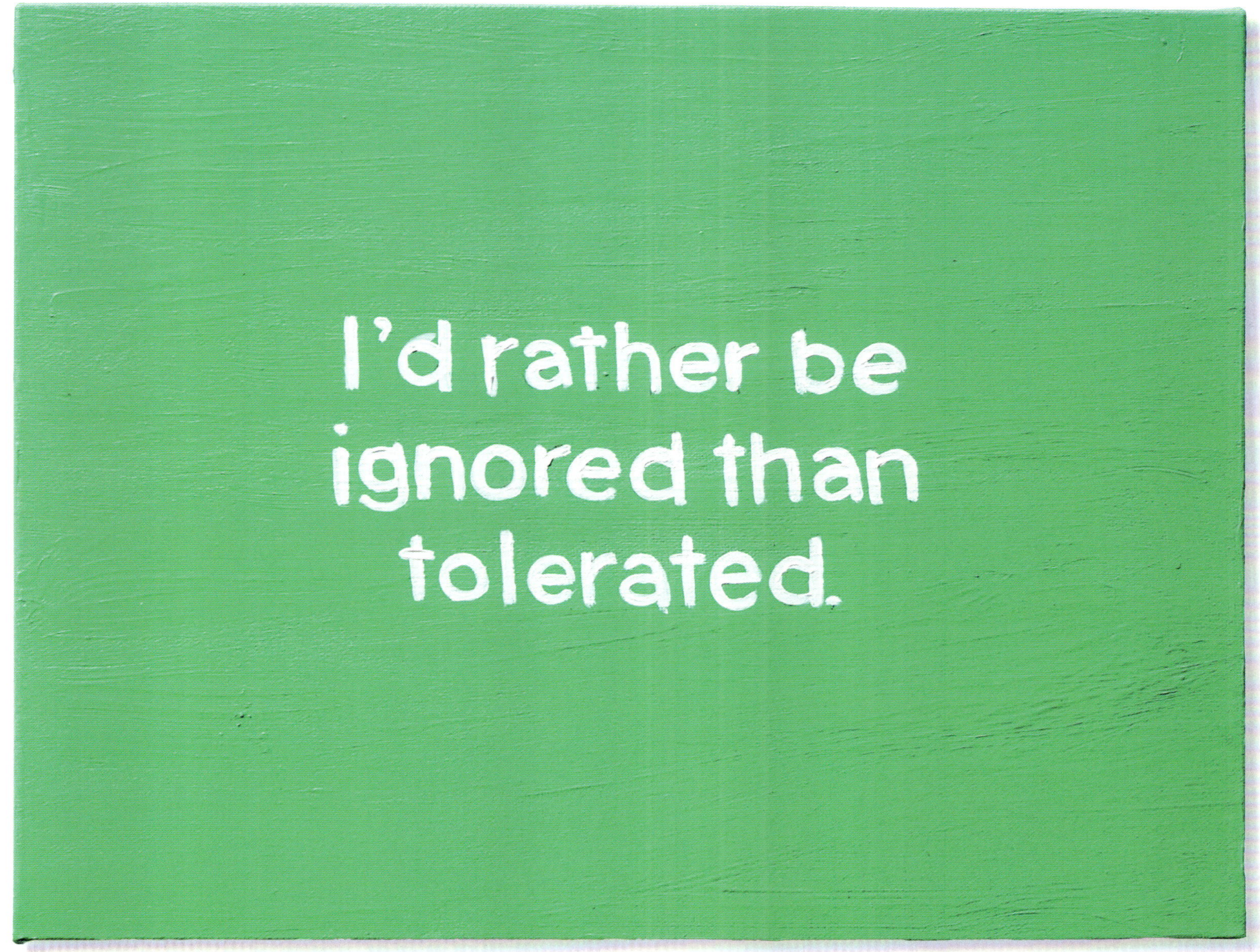

The Thoughts in My Head #86
2019
Acrylic on Canvas
11 x 14 inches

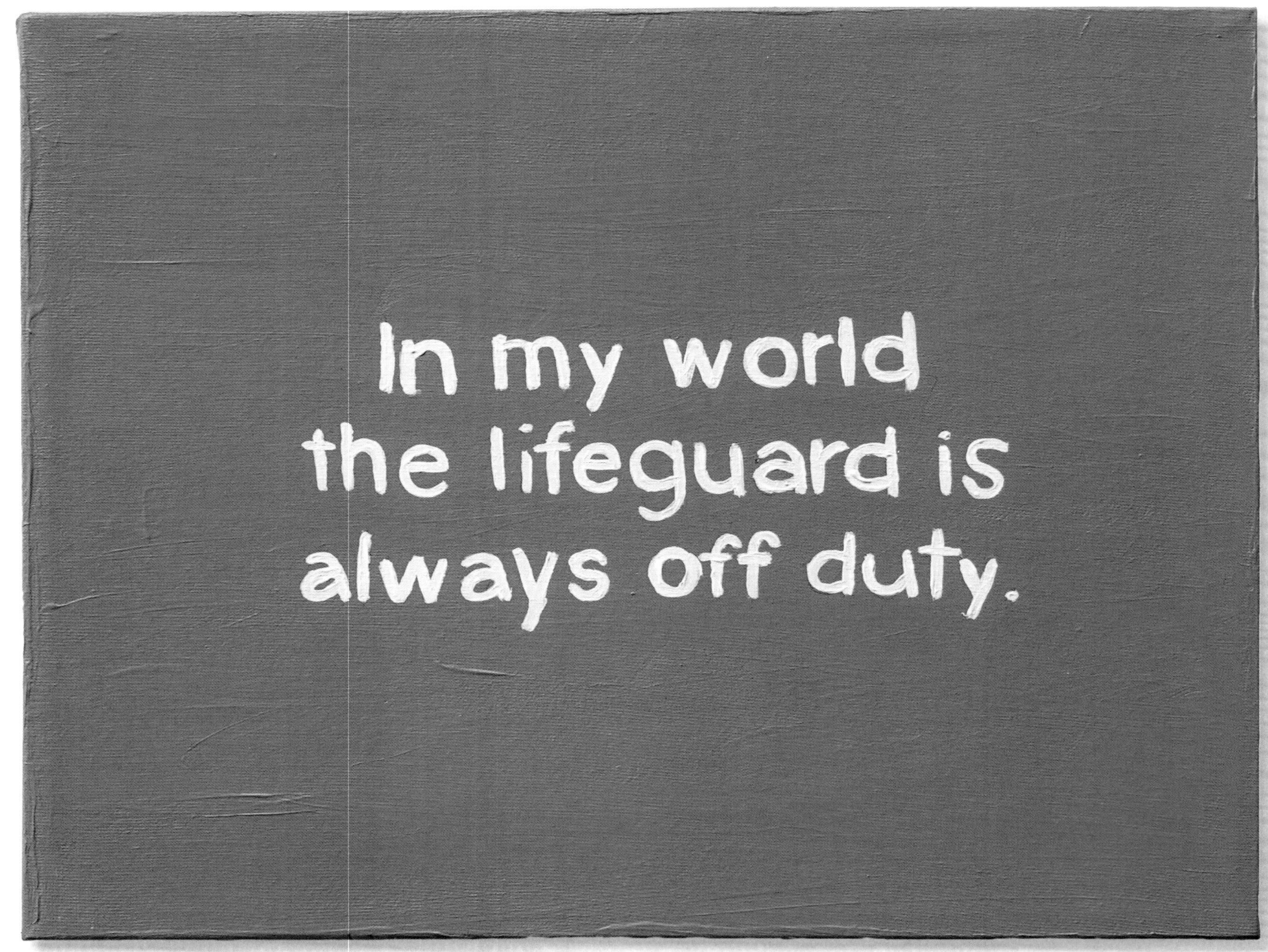

The Thoughts in My Head #87
2019
Acrylic on Canvas
11 x 14 inches

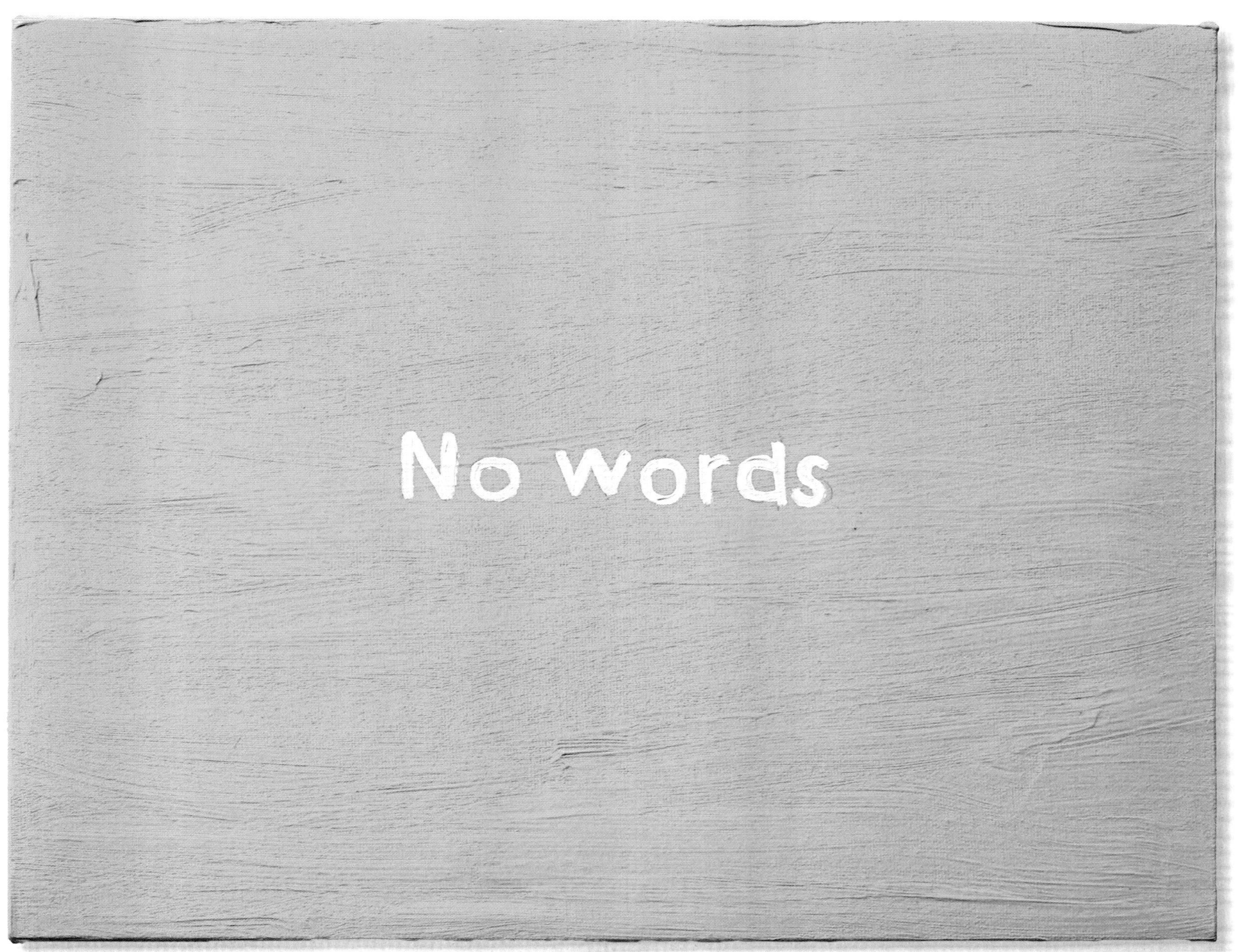

The Thoughts in My Head #88
2019
Acrylic on Canvas
11 x 14 inches

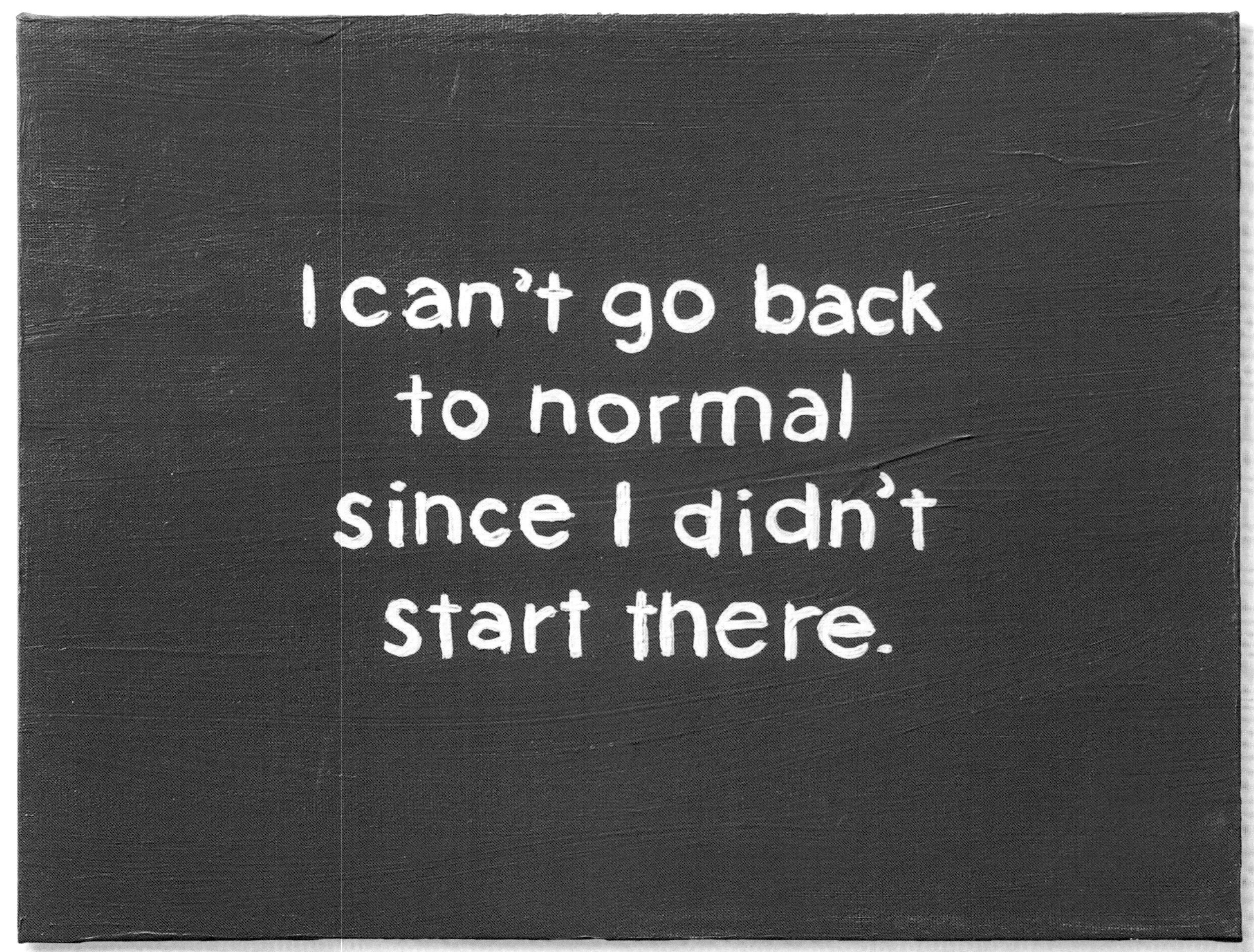

The Thoughts in My Head #89
2019
Acrylic on Canvas
11 x 14 inches

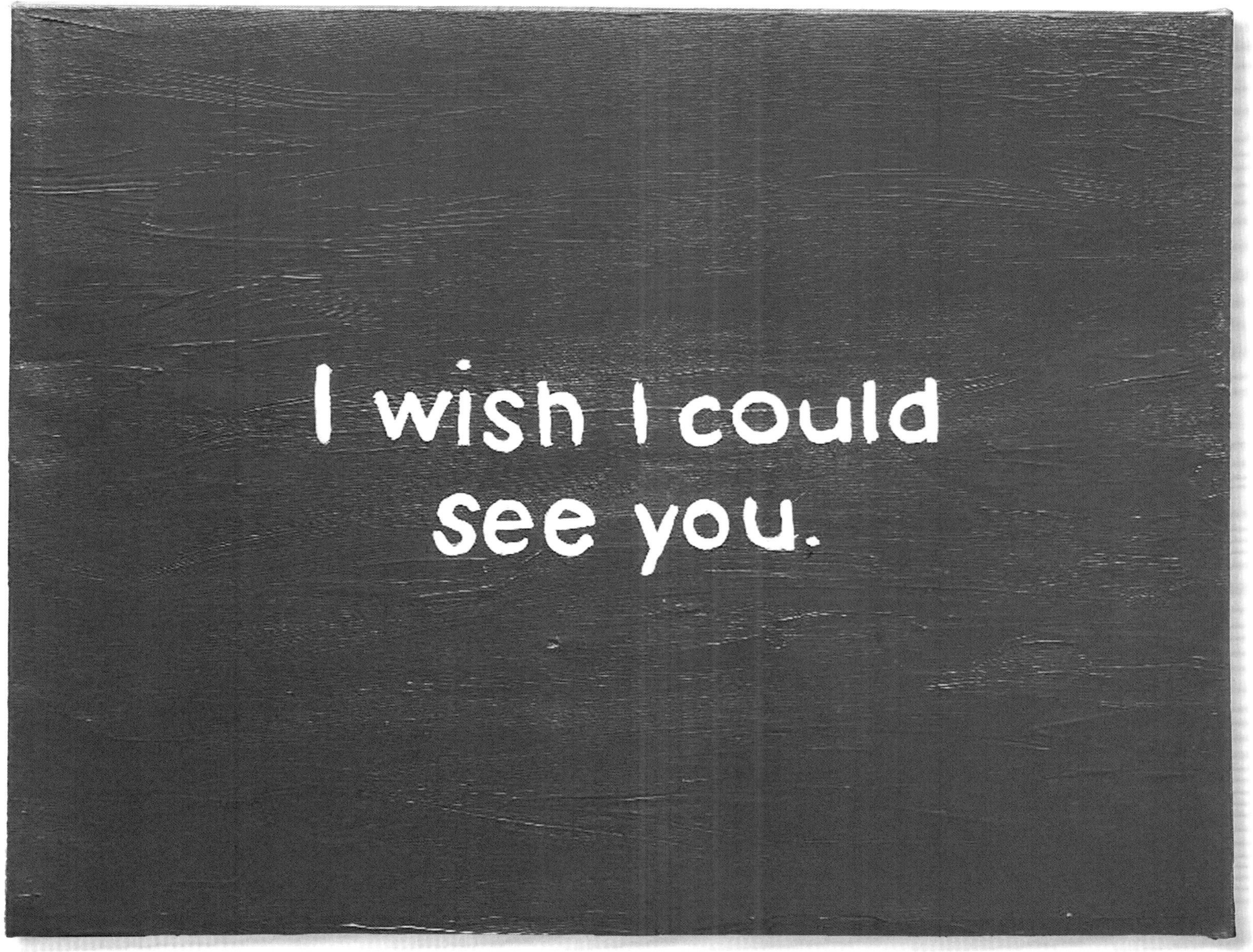

The Thoughts in My Head #90
2019
Acrylic on Canvas
11 x 14 inches

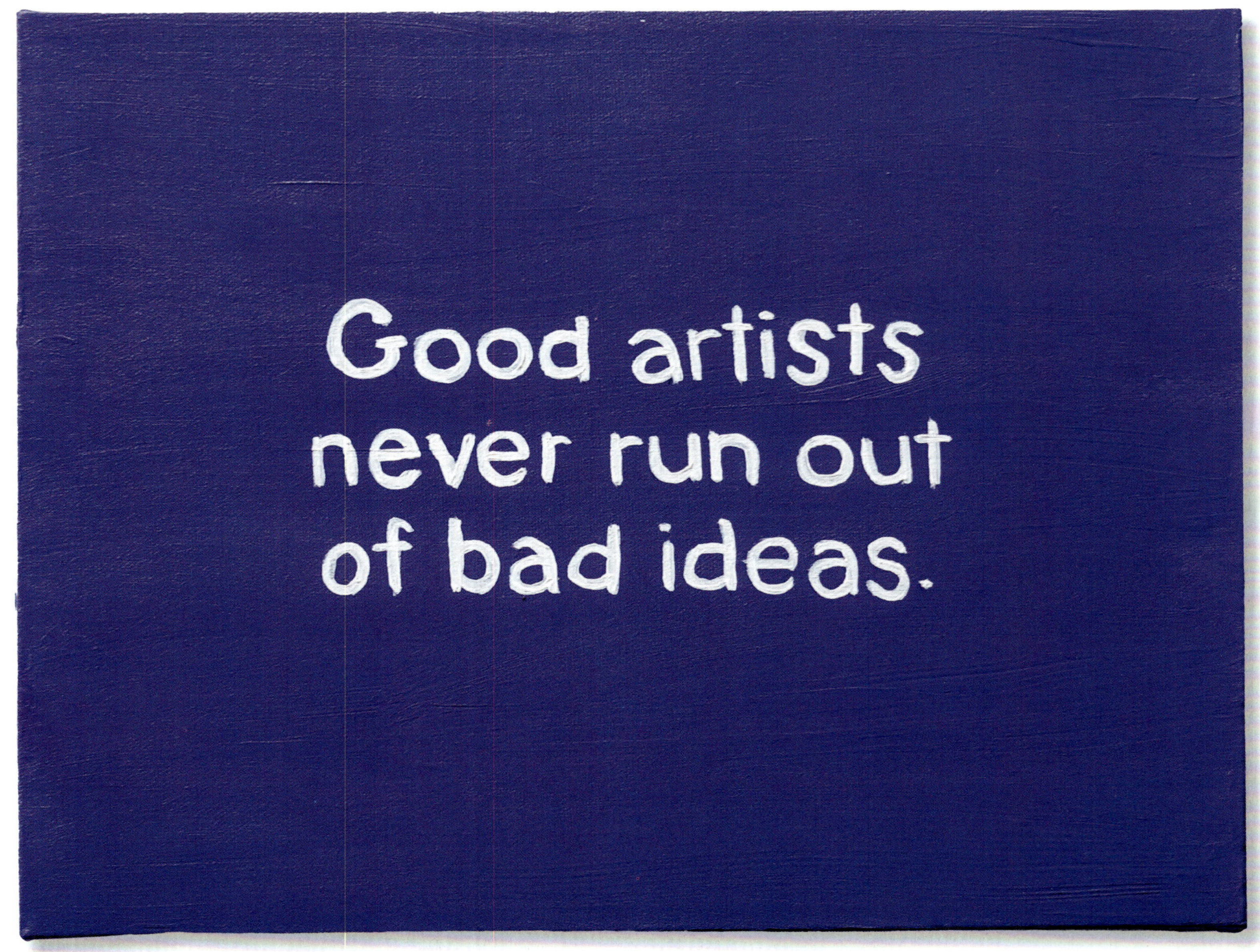

The Thoughts in My Head #91
2019
Acrylic on Canvas
11 x 14 inches

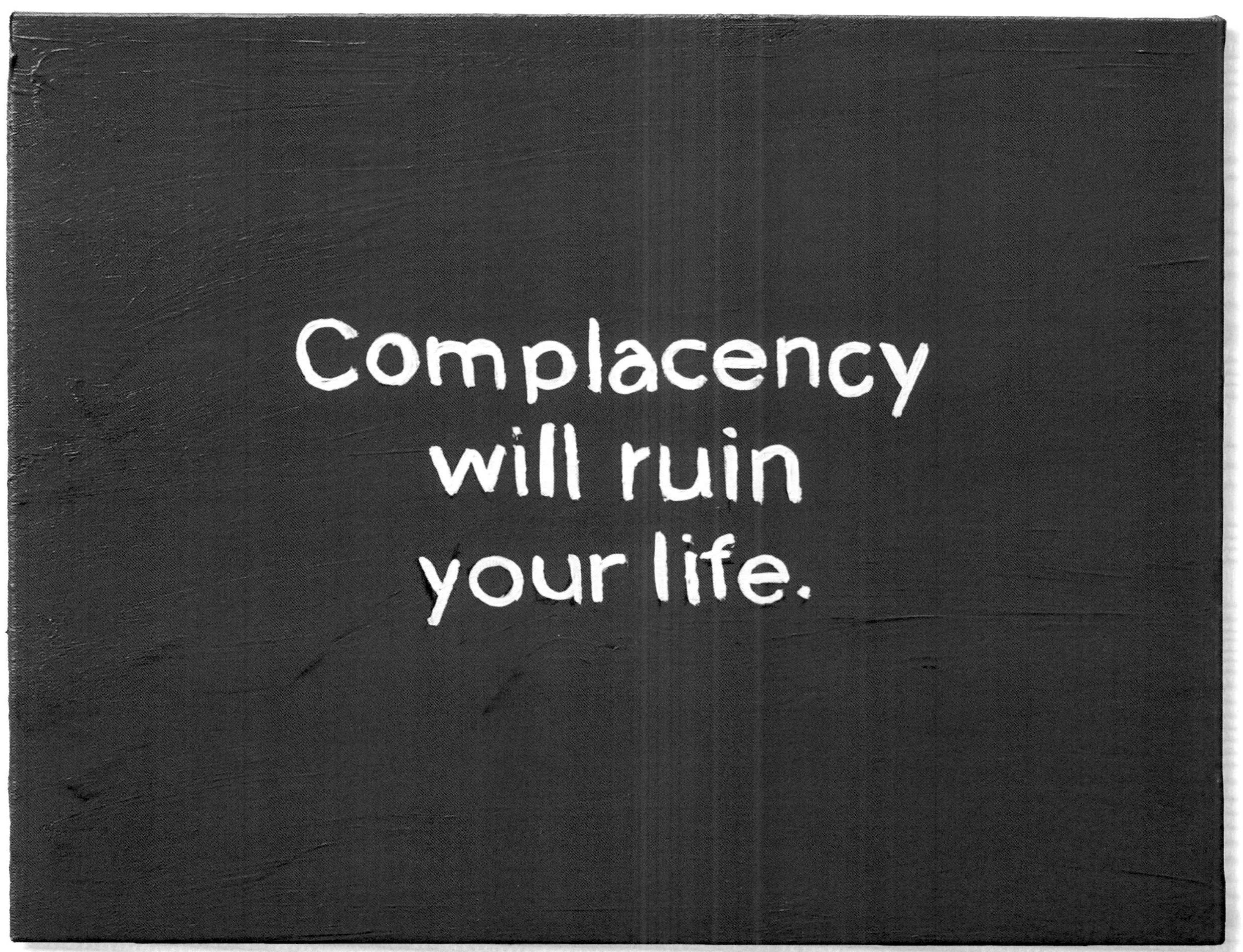

The Thoughts in My Head #92
2019
Acrylic on Canvas
11 x 14 inches

The Thoughts in My Head #93
2019
Acrylic on Canvas
11 x 14 inches

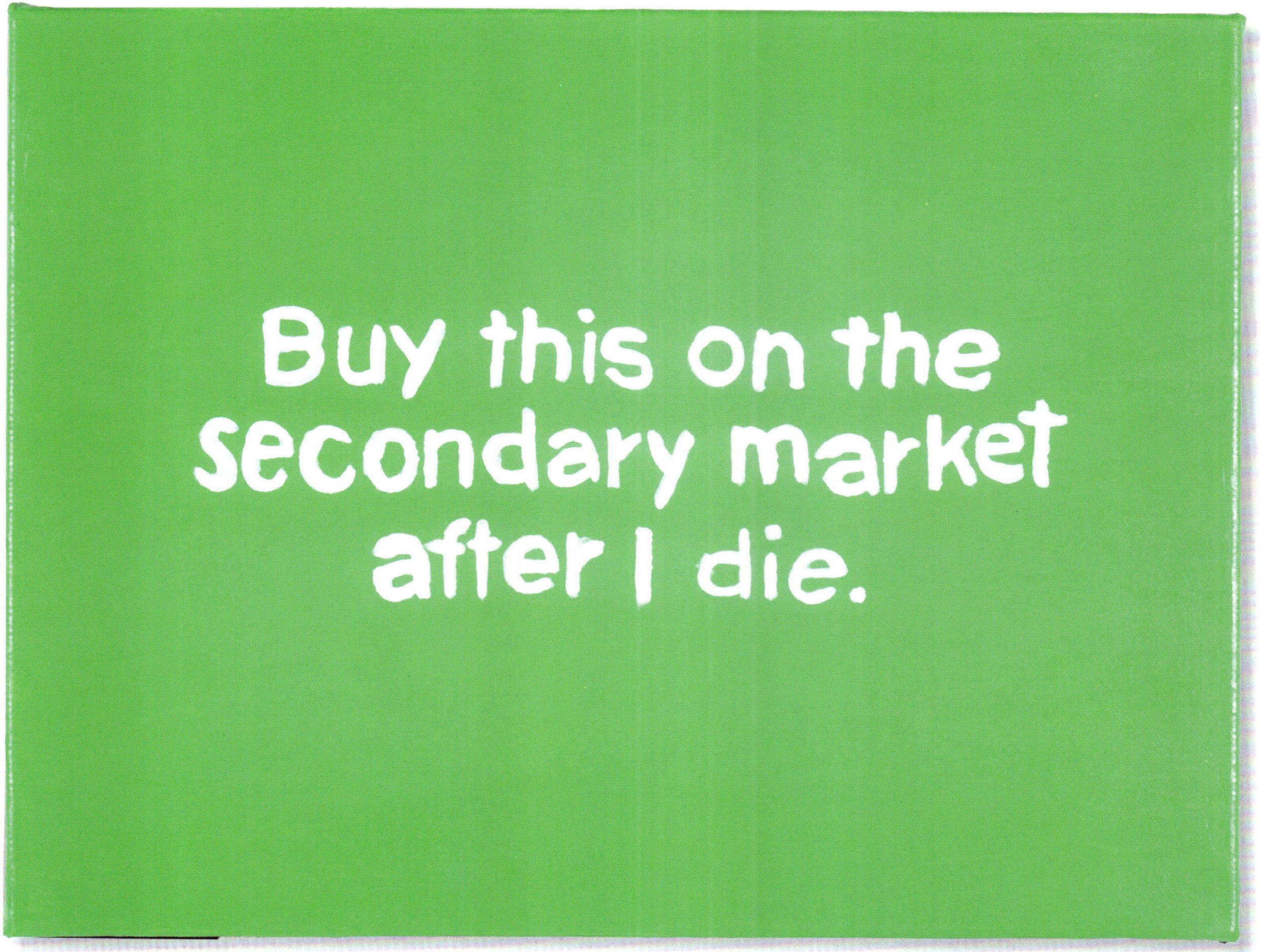

Buy this on the
secondary market
after I die.

The Thoughts in My Head #94
2019
Acrylic on Canvas
11 x 14 inches

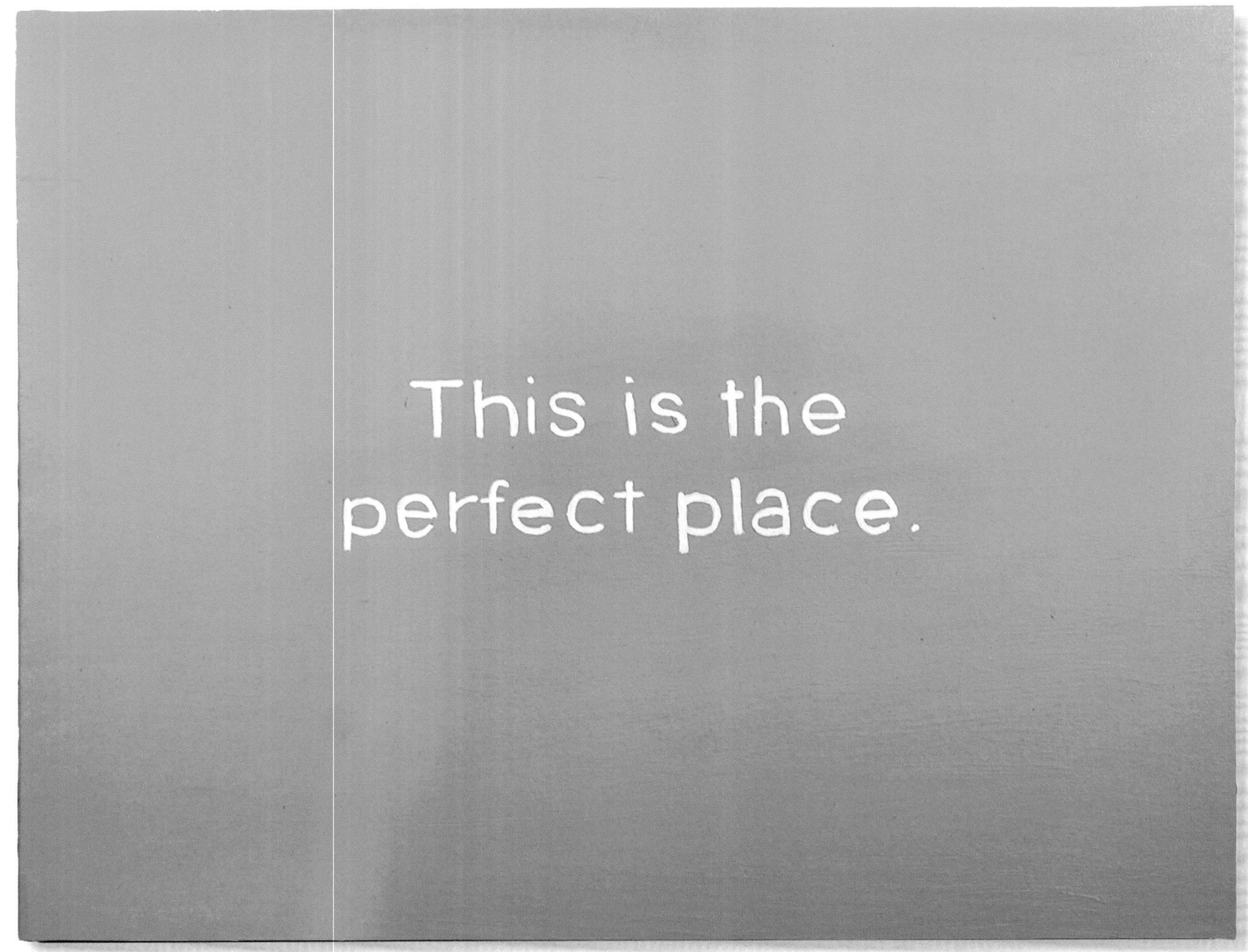

The Thoughts in My Head #95
2019
Acrylic on Canvas
11 x 14 inches

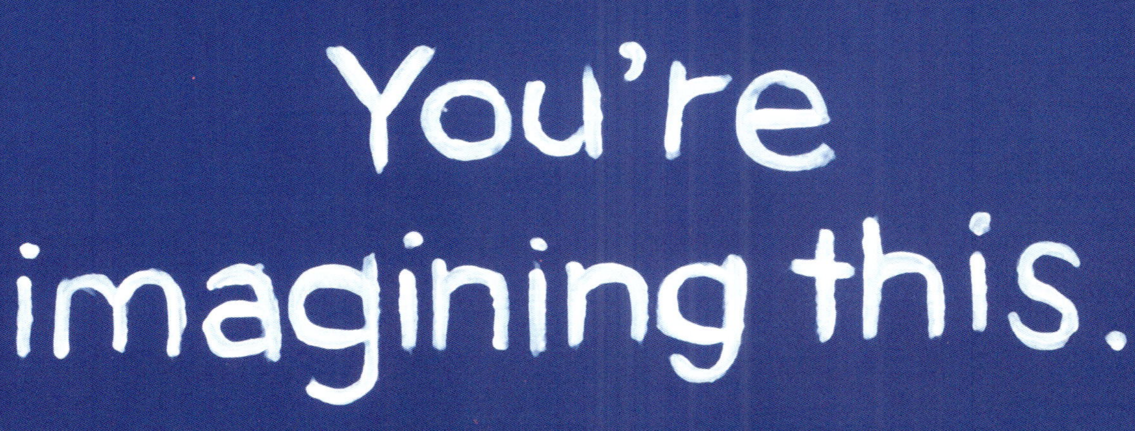

The Thoughts in My Head #96
2019
Acrylic on Canvas
11 x 14 inches

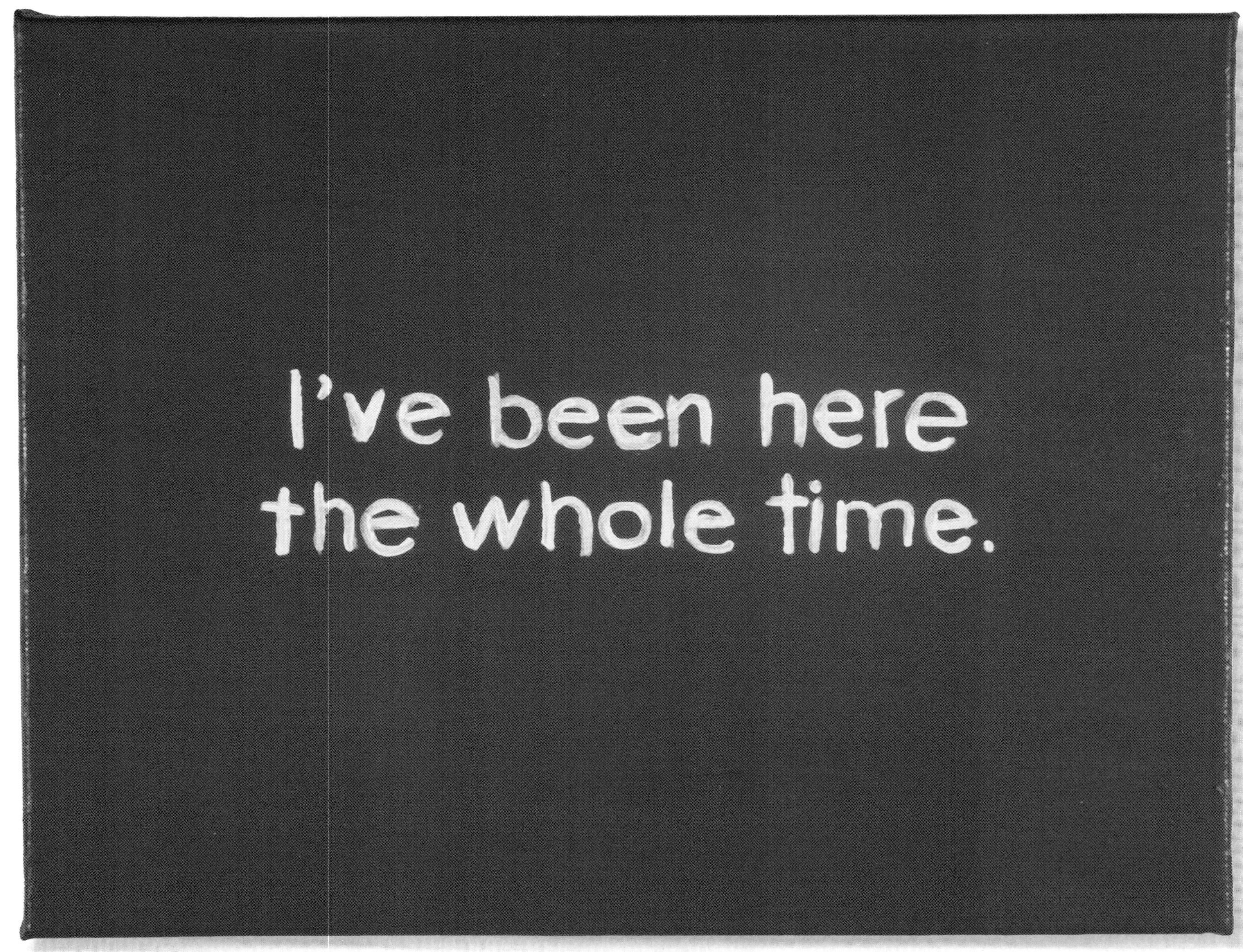

The Thoughts in My Head #97
2019
Acrylic on Canvas
11 x 14 inches

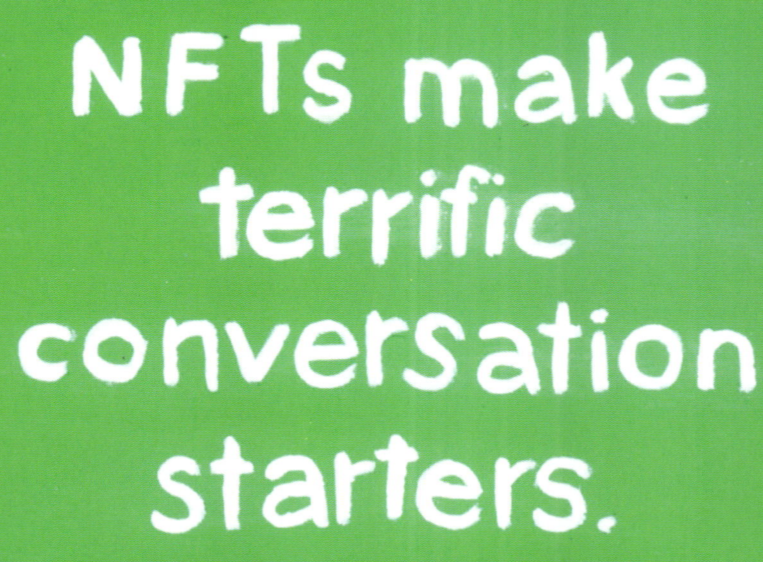

The Thoughts in My Head #98
2019
Acrylic on Canvas
11 x 14 inches

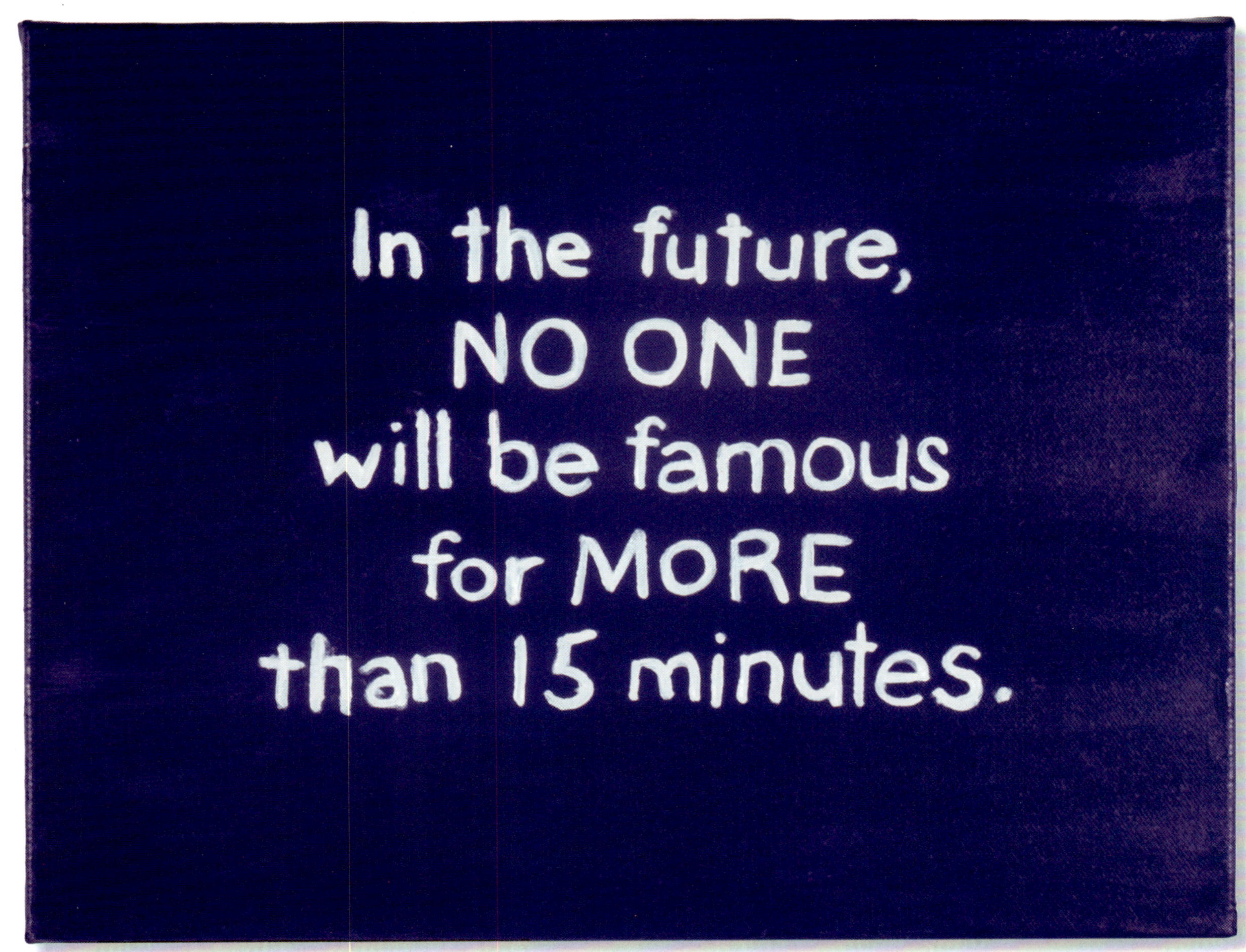

The Thoughts in My Head #99
2019
Acrylic on Canvas
11 x 14 inches

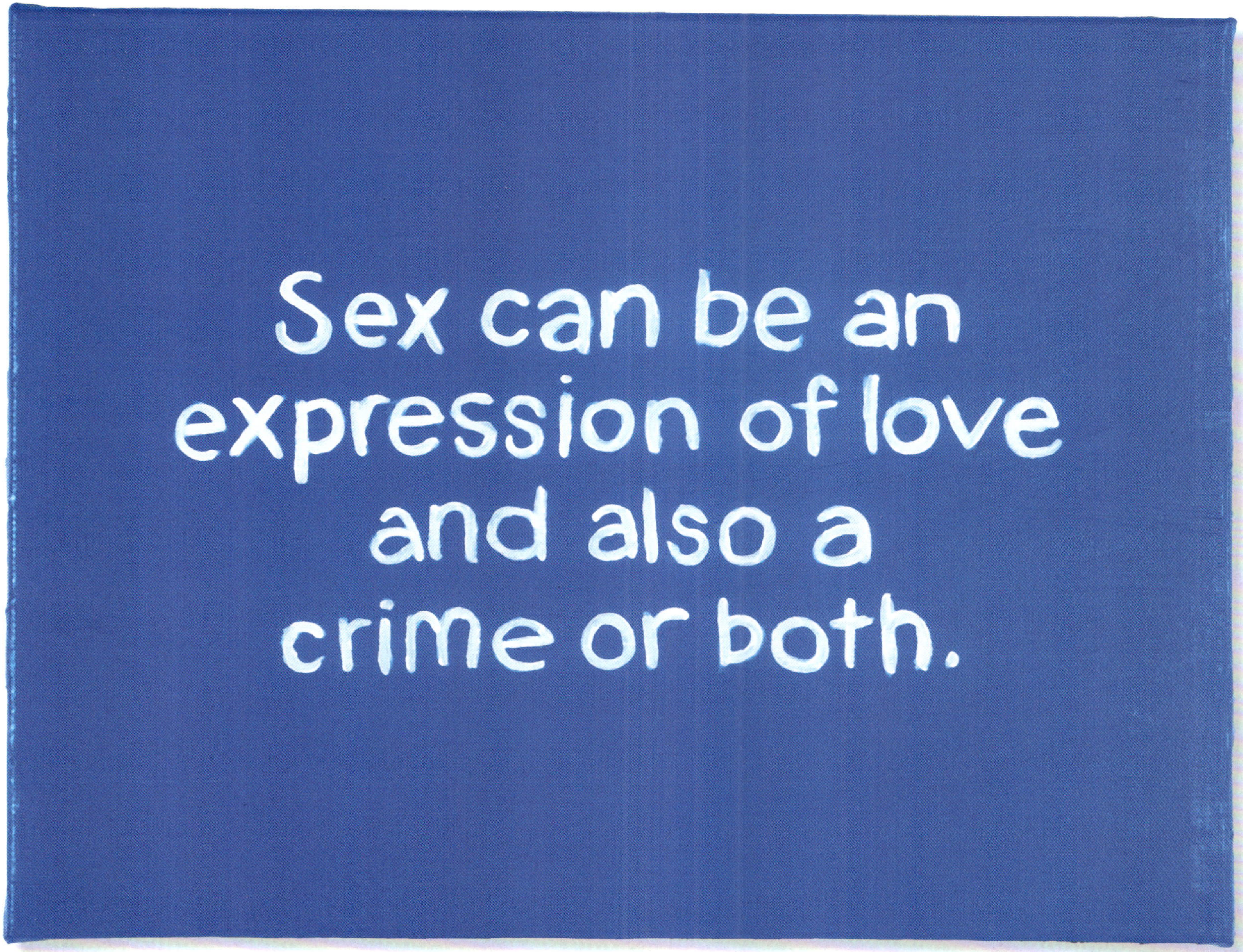

The Thoughts in My Head #100
2019
Acrylic on Canvas
11 x 14 inches

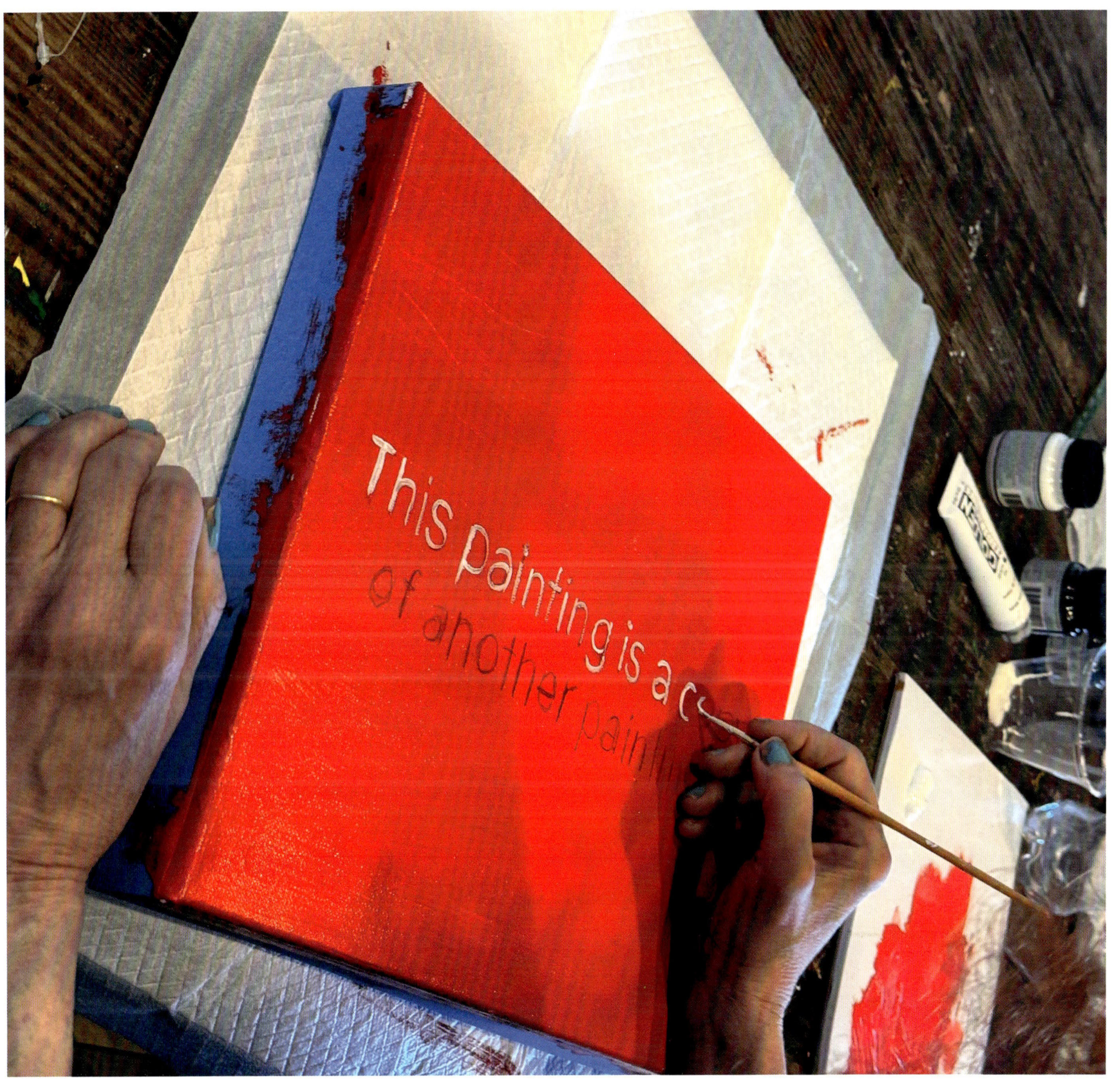

This painting is a c
of another pain

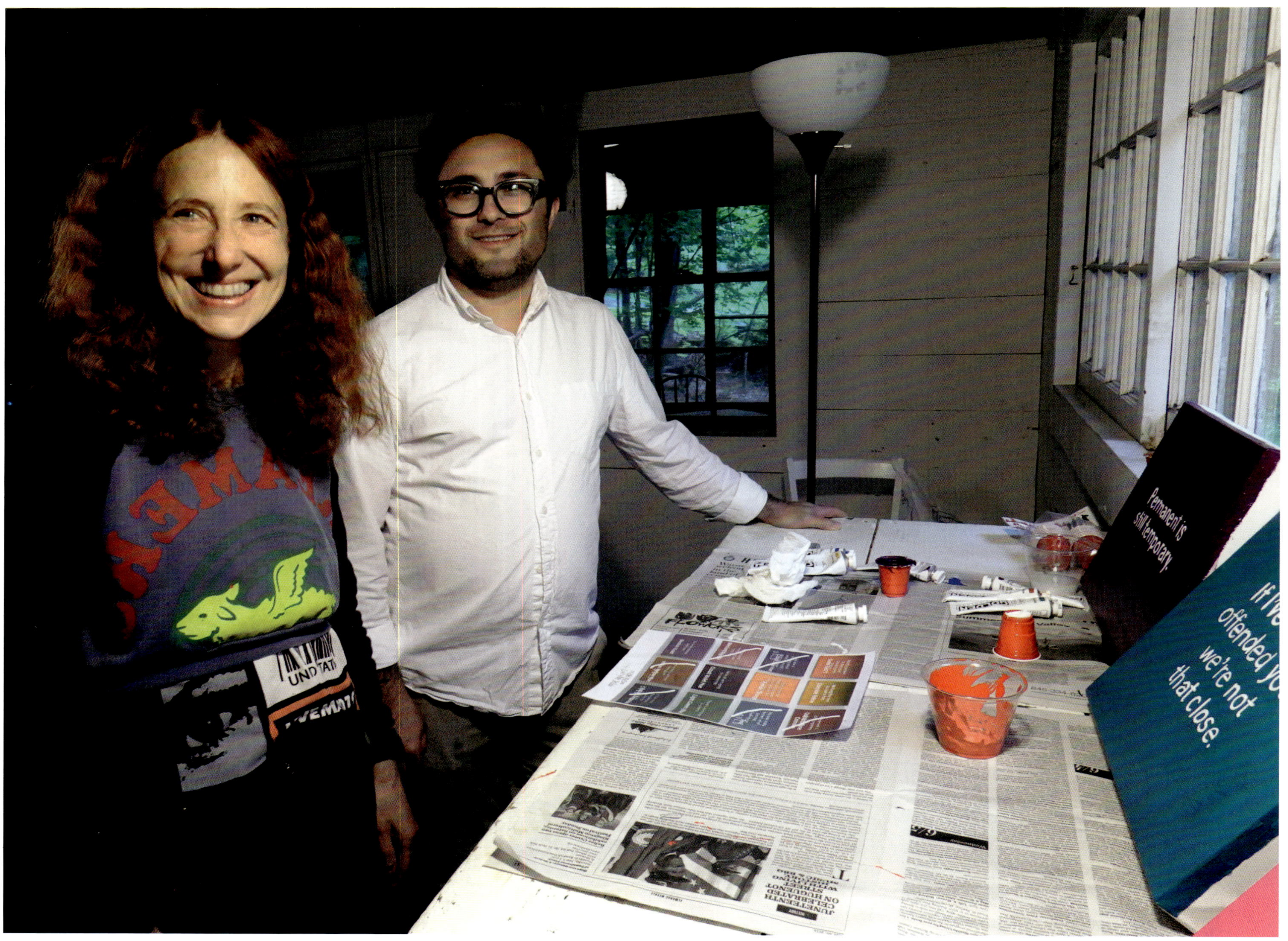

Permanent is still temporary.
If I've offended you we're not that close.

BIOGRAPHY

Lisa Levy's life and work blurs the lines between art and comedy—from conceptual artist to comedian and performer to host of her radio talk show, "Dr. Lisa Gives a Sh!t," on Radio Free Brooklyn. Levy's most notable character, Dr. Lisa, a self- proclaimed psychotherapist, emerged in 2001 in "Psychotherapy LIVE!" where she "analyzec" audience volunteers in 15-minute sessions. Levy is infamous for challenging the seriousness of art by sitting naked on a toilet for two days in a gallery satirizing Marina Abramović's famous MoMA performance, "The Artist Is Present." She currently curates a gallery inside the Brooklyn Comedy Collective to bring funny art by serious artists to a comedy space. Levy began her art career at age 3 ½ when her parents enrolled her in MoMA's children's school. She graduated Syracuse University with a degree in illustration and had a career as an advertising art director before deciding to devote herself full-time to her own art. Rooted firmly in concept and humor, her art can employ many forms, including performance, text, illustration, and painting, in various combinations.

Besides fine art and performance, Levy has had some unusual notable achievements. She's been on David Letterman's "Stupid Pet Tricks" with her bowling hamster, Bitey. She beat out over 12,000 entries in a national ad contest to win $83,000 for her ad campaign for Hebrew National. Levy was also crowned "Miss Subways 2017," which was produced by The City Reliquary.

Levy's work has been exhibited in numerous art fairs and galleries and has been covered with feature stories in publications suchas *The New York Times*, *The London Times*, *Time Out New York*, *The Daily News*, *The New York Post*, *Whitewall*, and *Dazed*, as well as prestigious art publications such as *ArtNet*, *Hyperallergic*, *Artforum*, and *ARTnews*.

Lisa Levy enjoying a studio visit with Jonathan Weiskopf,
VSOP Projects founder/director at Byrdcliffe Artist Residency, 2018
Photo: Phil Buehler

2024   ***Lisa Levy: The Thoughts in My Head*** (fall 2024), A monograph of 100 text paintings, 2011-2024, Published by Art Voices Books.
American Dream, Curated by Dasha Bazanova, Raynham Hall Museum, Long Island, NY
Skye Cleary Never Gets Old, Solo painting show by Skye Cleary, a sex doll that I use as an avatar. Includes a performance of the sex doll doing an artist talk with Marina Granger. The Untitled Space, NY, NY

2023   ***Dog House Gallery for Funny Art***, Opened a gallery within the Brooklyn Comedy Collective to exhibit work by artists that use humor in their work. Exhibit included solo exhibitions by Jen Catron + Paul Outlaw, David Kramer, Babak Ganjei and Shampoooty, Brooklyn, NY
Dr. Lisa Performs Therapy at the Artist Project Art Fair, Commissioned performance, Toronto, Canada
Reprise, Group show, VSOP Projects, Greenport, Long Island

2022   ***Playing with Dolls***, Collaboration with Sharilyn Neidhardt to present work through an avatar—a sex doll named Skye Cleary. SPRING/BREAK Art Show, NY, NY
Stand Up. Lie Down, Comedic performance, City Reliquary, Brooklyn, NY
2022 But What Do You Think of My Work? Collaboration with Sharilyn Neidhardt to present work through an avatar—a sex doll named Skye Cleary. Arcade Projects, Brooklyn, NY
Self-Reflection Mirrors, Art Market Hampton, VSOP Projects, Bridgehampton, NY

2021   ***Carry On***, Text bags, assorted bags exhibited and sold at Equity Gallery and Mother-in-Laws Haus, New York, NY, Kensington, NY
From The Archives: White Columns & 112 Greene Street 1970-2021, Selected from 1998. Curated by Matthew Higgs, NY, NY
The Thoughts in My Head #92-98, Art Market Hampton, VSOP Projects, Bridgehampton, NY

2020   ***The Thoughts in My Head #84-#92 Solo Show***, VSOP Projects, Greenport, NY

Dr. Lisa's Occupational Therapy Puzzle, Front Room Gallery LES, NY
Studio 54 Reject T-Shirt Reissue, Brooklyn Museum, NY
Lost Valentine, Friday Gallery, Brooklyn, NY

2019   ***But What Do You Think of My Work?*** Christopher Stout Projects, Satellite Art Fair, Brooklyn, NY
Psychotherapy LIVE!, Bad Theater Festival, Brooklyn, NY
Bridgehampton Art Fair, VSOP Projects, Bridgehampton, NY
Psychotherapy LIVE!, Chashama Gala NYC
Art on Paper fair, Mulherin and VSOP, NYC
Studio Mates, curated by Patricia Fabricant. Performance. Front Room, NYC

2018   ***Get My Stuff When I'm Dead***, Christopher Stout Projects, Solo Show, Brooklyn, NY
The Thoughts in My Head, VSOP Gallery, Solo Show, Greenport, NY
Transitioning Through Time in My Body, Live Performance curated by Coco Dolle, Catinca Tabacaru Gallery, NY, NY
The Thoughts in My Head 15'x10' wall, Permanent installation for IDEA1, curated by Ginger Shulick Porcella, San Diego, CA

2017   ***Winner Miss Subways Pageant 2017***, Pageant sponsored by The Riders Alliance and The City Reliquary, Brooklyn, NY
Take Us Lying Down, curated by Paul D'Agastino, Two-person show with artist Paul Gagner, SPRING/BREAK Art Fair, New York, NY
Fear Sharing, subway performance, New York, NY

2016   ***The Artist Is Humbly Present***, Stout Gallery, Brooklyn, NY

2015   ***Art Chopped***, Bruce High Quality Foundation, NY, NY
Couples Therapy with Dr. Lisa. TV Pilot, BRIC Arts, Brooklyn, NY
Dr. Lisa Gives a Sh*t. Weekly radio show, Radio Free Brooklyn, Brooklyn NY
If These Walls Could Talk. Jim Kempner Fine Art Gallery. New York, NY

2014   ***Lisa Levy Solo Project***, Pulse Miami, Schroeder Romero, Miami, Florida

What Makes You So Special: Dr. Lisa Investigates, Multimedia exhibition, Brooklyn Academy of Music
Everyone Loves A Winner, Auxiliary Projects, Brooklyn, NY.

2013 ***The Thoughts in My Head***, Hotel-wide installation, Yotel Hotel, NY, NY
ArtStar Editions, Artist prints. Curated by Chrissy Crawford. https://www.artstar.com/ Limited Edition Art
Why So Serious? Group show. Curated by Jen Hitchings, Weeknights Gallery, Brooklyn, NY

2012 ***Rockin' Mommy Love***, Performance where strangers sat on my lap and I got unconditional love. Momenta, Brooklyn, NY

2011 ***GalleryBeat Talk Show at The Brooklyn Museum***, Hosted by Paul H-O and Lisa Levy, The Brooklyn Museum, Brooklyn, NY
Crazy Lady, Curated by Jane Harris, Schroeder Romero and Shredder, NY, NY
What Matters Now, Curated by Debra Willis, Aperture Foundation Gallery, NY, NY
Psychotherapy with Alexander Melamed, Art of Healing Ministry, Northside Festival, Brooklyn NY
Analytic Visions. A group show of artwork by psychotherapists, Curated by Ron Lieber, Center for Modern Psychotherapy. New York, NY
I Like the Art World: An Evening of Performance and Creative Advice with Lisa Levy and Pablo Helguera
Dr. Lisa's Ego Challenge for Artists, Curated by Eric Doeringer, Elizabeth Foundation for the Arts, New York, NY

2010 ***Eliminating Obstacles to Creating Art #class***, Curated by Jen Dalton and William Powhida, Winkleman Gallery, NY, NY
Cooking with GalleryBeat, Co-host, live talk show, Pierogi 2000, Brooklyn, NY

2009 ***Stand Up. Lie Down***, Monthly performance at COMIX/Ochi's Lounge, NY, NY (up until May 2010)
Antidepressant Festival, The Brick Theater, Brooklyn, NY

2007 ***Red Carpet LIVE!*** Hosted the Oscar Party, Joe's Pub. NY, NY
IPO Program: Eric Doeringer/Emcee, Whitney Museum, NY, NY
My Kid Could've Done That, Video performance Scope Hamptons, Hamptons, NY

2004 ***Press Confrontation***, Creative Time: Freedom of Expression National, Monument, Foley Square. NY, NY
Psychotherapy Live! Edinburgh International Fringe Festival, Edinburgh, Scotland, UK

2002 ***Staged/Unstaged***, Curated by Lauri Firstenburg, Riva Gallery, New York, NY.
Psychotherapy LIVE! Monthly performance at Here Arts Center, Additional performances at Fez and the Knitting Factory, NY, NY. Since this project began, I have "psychoanalyzed" several thousand patients to date (2024). Well-known patients include: Amy Schumer, Joseph Gordon-Levitt, Laverne Cox, Eugene Mirman, Michael Musto, and many more.

2001 ***Prankster***, Curated by Lauren Ross, White Columns. NY, NY
Purloined, Curated by Christine Y. Kim, Artists' Space, NY, NY
Unstore, Solo exhibition, The Bronx Museum of the Arts, Bronx, NY
Yard Sale 2001, Curated by Rob Pruitt. Gavin Brown Enterprises, NY, NY

2000 ***Art Is Good Business***, Curated by Jenny Dixon. Solo takeover of the museum store, The Bronx Museum of the Arts, Bronx, NY

1999 ***The Time of Our Lives***, Commissioned souvenir tampons and Personalized Condom Rack, The New Museum Bookstore, NY, NY
Media Buy/Art Space Available, Window installation, Art in General, New York, NY

1998 ***Inventory, Group show***. Curated by Paul Ha, White Columns. New York, NY

1997 ***Take this Job and Shove It***. Created show concept and exhibited work. HereArt. New York, NY Hat Display. Cristinerose Gallery. New York, NY.

1996 ***National Juried Show*** curated by Eleanor Heartney of ***Art In America***. Phoenix Gallery. New York, NY
The Chastity Belt Show. HereArt. With Today Show appearance. New York, NY
First Exposure Series. GenArt, New York, NY
The L-Word Show. Curated by Larry Walczak. Gallery 473, New York, NY

SELECTED BIBLIOGRAPHY

Benzine, Vittoria, See Inside a Solo Exhibition of Works by an Artist's Sex Doll, Artnet, March 28, 2024

Publika, Liz, Event Spotlight: The Untitled Space presents SKYE CLEARY NEVER GETS OLD, Art Publika, March 14, 2024

Davidson, Sarah, Artist Project Toronto will host free therapy sessions with Dr. Lisa Levy, Toronto Guardian, April 10, 2023

Sachdeva, Maanya, Marina Abramović says she will 'definitely not' be dying for her art, The Independent, September 23, 2023

Kelley, Lyndsay, After Eating: Metabolizing the Arts, The MIT Press, 2023

Cascone, Sarah, See inside Spring/Break, the Indie Art fair That Took over Ralph Lauren's Offices with Edgy, Outrageous and Surprisingly Affordable Art, ArtNet, September 8, 2023

Johnson, Ros, Comedy As Therapy: Five Notable Examples, Minding Therapy, September 28, 2022

Cascone, Sarah, Editors' Picks: 14 Things Not to Miss in the Virtual Art World This Week, ArtNet, April 20, 2020

Frost, Natasha, The Miss Subways Pageant Charted the Highs and Lows of 20th-Century Feminism, Atlas Obscura, Oct. 4, 2017

Nakamura, Go, New York Subways Pageant Struts Back Into NYC Spotlight, New York Daily News, Sept. 29, 2017

Editors, Spring/Break Art Show Highlights – Armory Arts Week, Untitled Magazine, Mar. 2, 2017

Laster, Paul, Occupying Offices: Independent vs. Spring/Break, Whitehot Magazine, March 2017

Dawn, Cassidy Graves, Art This Week, Bedford and Bowery, October 31, 2017

Bahamondes, Bianca, Artist Gives Away her Belongings at Bushwick Exhibit in Preparation for Death, Secret NYC, November 9, 2017

Rakewell, Now it's Cate Blanchett's turn to spoof Marina Abramović, Apollo Magazine, Aug. 11, 2018

Halle, Howard, Can do spirit: Artist to sit naked on a toilet in a 10-hour performance, Time Out New York, Jan.16, 2016

Munroe, Cait, Artist Will Sit Naked on a Toilet In Performance Against Marina Abramović's Vanity, ArtNet, Jan. 22, 2016

Bokar, Neha, Artist To Sit Naked On Pot To Protest Against 'Bulls**t' Contemporary Art World! India Times, Jan. 24, 2016

Crocker, Lizzie, Performance art goes to the toilet in Brooklyn of course, The Daily Beast, Jan. 29, 2016

Arsen, Jan, Lisa Levy Pushes Borders of Performance Art Out of Protest - And We Wonder if the Toilet is Just a Prop? Widewalls, Jan. 22, 2016

Sisly, Dominic, An artist is about to sit naked on a toilet for two days, Dazed Digital, Jan 22, 2016

Anelli, Marco, An artist is about to sit naked on a toilet for two days, Dangerous Minds, January, 21, 2016

Moore, Christopher, Artist Lisa Levy mocks pretentiousness by sitting naked on a toilet at a Brooklyn gallery, New York Daily News, January 22, 2016

Crocker, Lizzie, Performance Art Goes to the Toilet—in Brooklyn, Of Course, The Daily Beast, January 19, 2016

Kentish, Francesca, Artist to sit naked on a toilet for 2 days to protest against the bullsh*t art world, *Metro UK*, Jan. 22, 2017

Steadman, Ryan, Naked Artist Rides the Porcelain Throne to Protest Art World BS, *Observer*, January 22, 2017

Embuscado, Rain, A Brief History of Poop-Related Art, *ArtNet*, May 2, 2016

Shen, Holly, What makes you so special, BAM Archives, BAM Archives, February, 12, 2015

Munro, Cait, 20 Standout Works at New York's Affordable Art Fair, Under $1,000 and Under $5,000, *ArtNet*, April 4, 2014
    New York Gallery Beat: 5 Critics Review 14 Shows, ArtNet, April 24, 2014
    Chrissy Crawford's Contemporary Curated Picks. Sotheby's.com, June 12, 2014

Hoffman, Meredith, Artist Paints Therapy Patients' 'Psychological Portraits,' *DNA Info*, August 1, 2012

Ortiz, Matthew. *"An Artist Creates Psychotherapy."* Psychology Tomorrow Magazine. September 2012.

Brooks, Katherine, "Artist Dr. Lisa Levy Performs Free Psychotherapy Session In 'The Thoughts in Your Head.'" HuffPost. August, 8, 2012.

Robinson, Walter. "Art Show as Think Tank." *ArtNet*, February 18, 2010

McLaughlin, Brendon, "Comedians Become Patients at a Monthly Show." Punchlinemagazine.com, January 21, 2009.

Alexis Soloski, "Voice Choices." The Village Voice, October 3-10, 2007. p. 23

Davis, Ben, Scope Hampered? *ArtNet*, July 14, 2006

Dolan, James, First stage of madness, *The London Times*, August 21, 2004

Boxer, Sarah, A Shrink with Stage Presence, The New York Times, July 27, 2002

Musto, Michael, "La Dolce Musto." *The Village Voice*. August 4, 2002. p. 16

Hanahan, James "Beyond Therapy," *The Village Voice*, Aug. 21, 2001.

Finch, Charlie, Opening Night, ArtNet, September, 6, 2001

Cotter, Holland, "A Flock of Fledglings Testing Their Wings," *The New York Times*, August 1, 1997. p.26 (section C).

"Artist in the Marketplace Seventeenth Annual Exhibition," The Bronx Museum of the Arts, exhibition catalogue, Spring 1997

Stern, Aimee, Selling yourself on Madison Ave, The New York Times, October 1, 1989

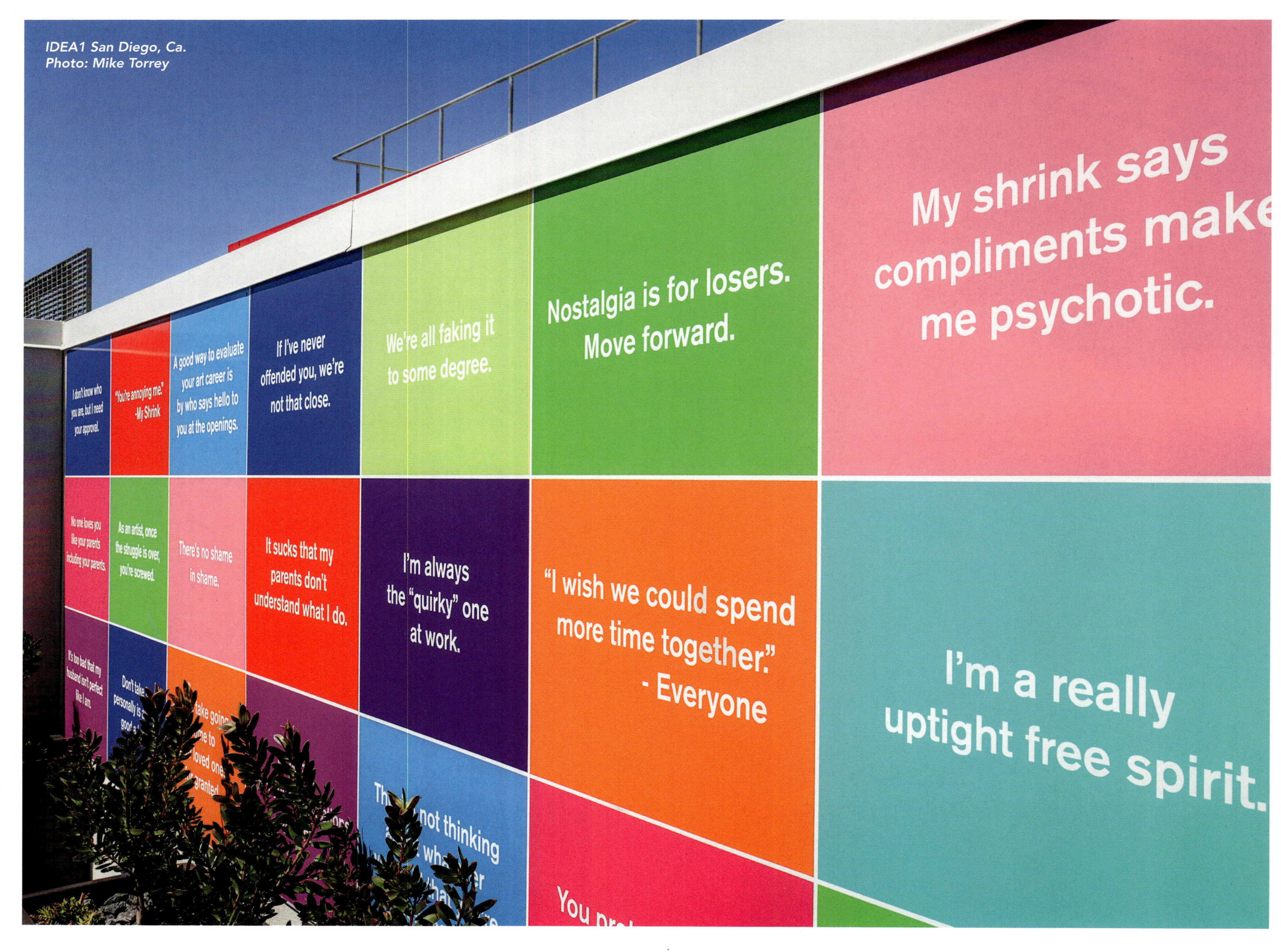
IDEA1 San Diego, Ca.
Photo: Mike Torrey
I don't know who you are, but I need your approval.
"You're annoying me."
-My Shrink
A good way to evaluate your art career is by who says hello to you at the openings.
If I've never offended you, we're not that close.
We're all faking it to some degree.
Nostalgia is for losers. Move forward.
My shrink says compliments make me psychotic.
No one loves you like your parents including your parents.
As an artist, once the struggle is over, you're screwed.
There's no shame in shame.
It sucks that my parents don't understand what I do.
I'm always the "quirky" one at work.
"I wish we could spend more time together."
- Everyone
It's too bad that my husband isn't perfect like I am.
Don't take personally is
I'm a really uptight free spirit.
You

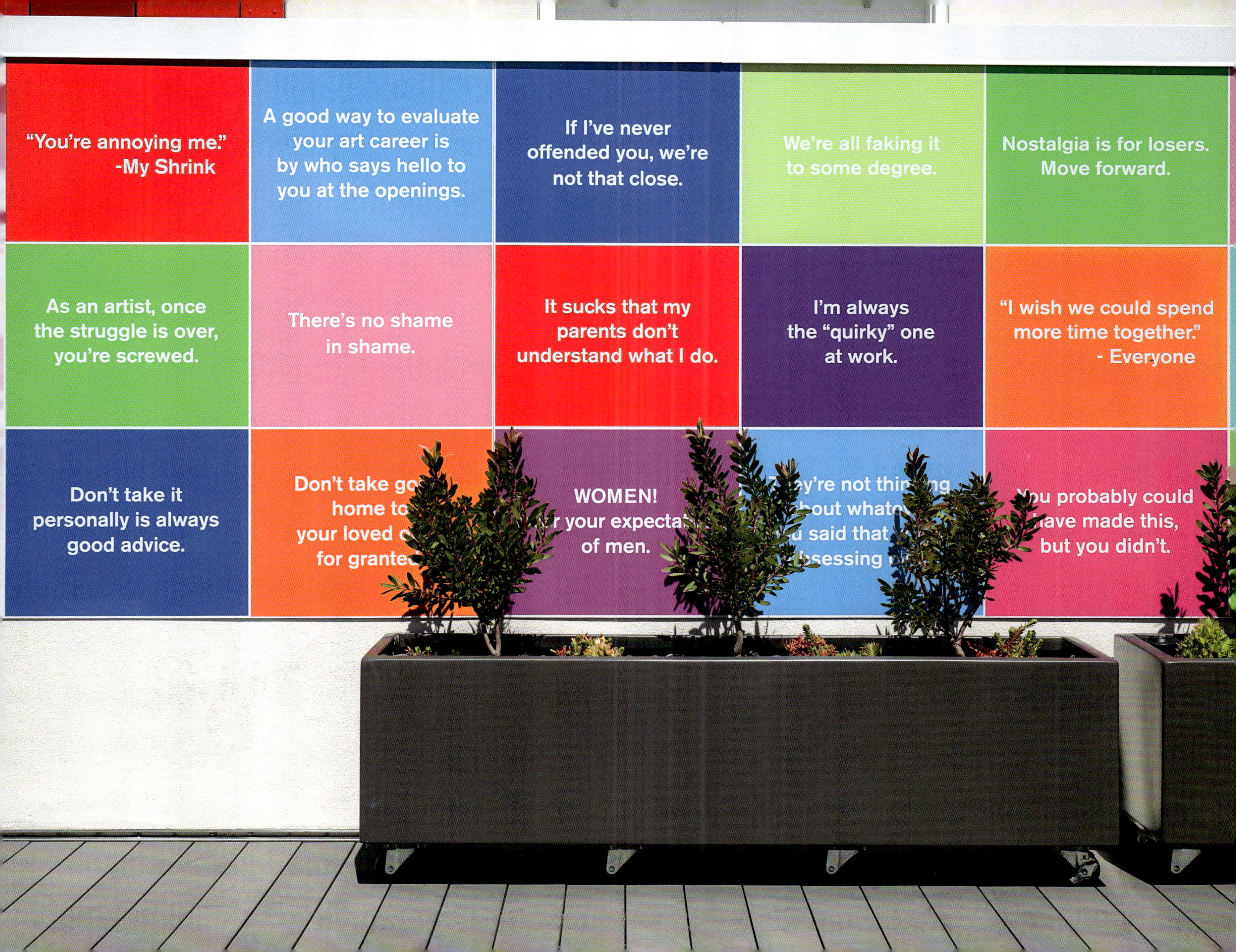

"You're annoying me." -My Shrink
A good way to evaluate your art career is by who says hello to you at the openings.
If I've never offended you, we're not that close.
We're all faking it to some degree.
Nostalgia is for losers. Move forward.
As an artist, once the struggle is over, you're screwed.
There's no shame in shame.
It sucks that my parents don't understand what I do.
I'm always the "quirky" one at work.
"I wish we could spend more time together." - Everyone
Don't take it personally is always good advice.
Don't take go home to your loved for granted
WOMEN! r your expecta of men.
y're not thin out what u said that bsessing
You probably could ave made this, but you didn't.